The
Soul Mate
myth

The

Soul
Mate
myth

A 3-Step Plan for *Finding* **REAL** *Love*

Jean Cirillo, PhD

Avon, Massachusetts

Published by
Adams Media, a division of F+W Media, Inc.
57 Littlefield Street, Avon, MA 02322. U.S.A.
www.adamsmedia.com

ISBN 10: 1-4405-1271-X
ISBN 13: 978-1-4405-1271-1
eISBN 10: 1-4405-2666-4
eISBN 13: 978-1-4405-2666-4

Printed in the United States of America.

10 9 8 7 6 5 4 3 2 1

Library of Congress Cataloging-in-Publication Data
is available from the publisher.

This publication is designed to provide accurate and authoritative information
with regard to the subject matter covered. It is sold with the understanding
that the publisher is not engaged in rendering legal, accounting, or other
professional advice. If legal advice or other expert assistance is required, the
services of a competent professional person should be sought.

—From a *Declaration of Principles* jointly adopted by a Committee of the
American Bar Association and a Committee of Publishers and Associations

Many of the designations used by manufacturers and sellers to distinguish their
product are claimed as trademarks. Where those designations appear in this
book and Adams Media was aware of a trademark claim, the designations have
been printed with initial capital letters.

This book is available at quantity discounts for bulk purchases.
For information, please call 1-800-289-0963.

Dedication

This book is dedicated to my late father, Carmine Cirillo, who passed away three years ago, while I was visiting him in Las Vegas. He was always behind me, to provide support, intellectual guidance, and love in all of my endeavors.

Acknowledgments

My profound gratitude is extended to everyone who made this book possible:

Janet Rosen, my agent at Sheree Bykofsky and Associates, who recommended me for this project, and worked alongside me as my loyal teammate from start to finish.

Victoria Sandbrook, my acquisitions editor at Adams Media, who brought me on, encouraged me, and led the way through twists, turns, and bumps along the road.

Katie Corcoran Lytle, my development editor at Adams Media, who suggested direction and worked hard to put the finishing touches on this book.

Cynthia Cedano, who worked tirelessly alongside me to meet deadlines in producing the final product.

Julia Austin, whose skilled writing and editing abilities did much to enhance the book's readability and style.

Ellis Pailet, national entertainment lawyer from New Orleans, whose excellent advice guided me along the way.

Clients, friends, family, and all those persons who, throughout my life, provided the material and fuel that are the lifeblood of this work.

Contents

Introduction

Ladies, we've been tricked. From fairy tales at bedtime to Hollywood's blockbuster hits, we've been told that there's a one-and-only soul mate for each of us, and that he'll be a perfect man—and that you'll have the perfect relationship. And what's worse: we've started believing it. After all, you *deserve* something perfect, right? You work hard, you love hard, and you've been waiting a long time for the fireworks and mixtapes and roses every anniversary. So why don't you have it yet?

No, it's not that you're just impatient. And no, I'm not going to tell you that you'll find happiness if you just lower your standards. But the endless searching and predictable backfiring and constant disappointment *does* need to end, and you're the only one who can turn this all around.

If you're still wondering if any of this applies to you, just answer the next few questions:

- Have you ever crossed a guy off your list after one date?
- Do you have trouble finding someone *to* date because you cross guys off your list so quickly?
- Have you ever left someone because he wouldn't change?
- Are you afraid of committing too soon?
- Are you with a guy everyone loves—except you?
- Do men usually disappoint you once you get to know them?

If you answered yes to more than one, it's likely that you are working against yourself in some way or another. At some point, when you had been disappointed by too many guys, you decided to protect yourself from that pain and started setting up every man you meet for failure. After all, if he was such a loser/deadbeat/infidel/jerk/whatever, then you're better off without him, right? So you set guys up so they had no choice but to end up looking like all of those terrible things in your eyes. Undoing the damage won't be easy either: even the biology of your brain plays a part in keeping you from finding the right love at the right time! So you have to start at the very beginning.

The good news is that there is no such thing as a one-and-only soul mate for each person. Recent research indicates that the odds of finding someone out there who is biologically and chemically compatible are actually one in eleven! That's right ladies, the odds are much better than you thought. It just might be your method of looking that is lessening those odds.

This book will strip away everything you think is necessary in love—from the celluloid glamour to your own high expectations—and show you what is *actually* necessary for a lasting relationship. You'll look at what you think love is and get to the heart of your outlook on men and romance—and yourself. When you find the secret triggers that tell you to back off, you'll learn which ones to keep and which ones are holding you back. You'll learn what can be compromised, and what values you should never compromise. And, if you're a single lady who's having trouble dating, there's a whole appendix just for you where you'll learn how to use your natural charm to put yourself out there. You'll also learn how to take control of your priorities, hopes, and fears so that you can learn which to keep, which to ditch, which are reasonable, and which are just hindering you from finding love. You will rebuild your roadmap to finding a fulfilling love life.

You *are* hardwired to have long, happy, fulfilling relationships with others. You *are* deserving of a committed, powerful relationship. You just have to let yourself find it.

- -

REALITY CHECK:

A Toolkit for Understanding How Bad You've Got It

In this part you will learn to recognize your expectations and determine which ones are realistic and which are unrealistic; see the role your brain and your nervous system play in determining your choice of a romantic partner; and you'll learn to recognize—and begin to overcome—the fears that act as barriers to finding real love, keeping you stuck in the soul mate myth. Consider this first part your break up with the mythical man. When you break up with a boyfriend, you naturally try to understand what you could have done differently, what he could have done differently, and eventually you come to accept the fact that the two of you were simply not meant to be. In this first part you will learn why you and the mythical soul mate are not meant to be and why that is perfectly okay.

CHAPTER 1

Great Expectations

If you look at some couples who have been together since they were very young, you probably recognize dynamics that, in your long years of dating, you've learned that you would *never* want in a relationship. Because you *have* been out there. You *have* tested the waters. Chances are you have learned more about what you want from a relationship, which is an advantage . . . to a point. Your standards may have actually gotten *too* high, without you even realizing it. Yes, you've worked too damned hard and are too great of a catch to bend on what you want. But you can shout, "I'm a catch!" from the rooftops and it doesn't change the fact that you're single. Obviously, something isn't working.

Here's the thing: some of your expectations are probably valid. You didn't pull them out of thin air. You've taken note of what really didn't work in past relationships and what did. By drawing on past relationships, you protect yourself from getting into another similar, unsuccessful one. So don't write off everything you've determined to be good or bad in a relationship.

But there's a good chance that some of your expectations aren't valid, and it's time for you to get real about what's realistic to expect from a mate, what you'd like to get out of your relationship, and what you consider a deal-breaker. After all, the more you can compromise—without compromising yourself—and relearn what you *should* expect from your partner, the happier you'll be. Yes, I said relearn, because unfortunately, you may have just gotten a fractured and even flawed education when it came to building expectations for a relationship.

Where Do Those Expectations Come From?

Throughout your life, you've been constantly bombarded with ideas of what love *should* look like. It's the subject of countless novels, poems, songs, and movies. No doubt, you've fallen in love with many charismatic characters—from your favorite teen idol to that hot guy at the gym to *Pride and Prejudice*'s Mr. Darcy— over the years and it's easy to weave the best of each of those guys into a truly demanding set of qualifications that make up Mr. Right. He never panics in a stressful situation. He thinks it's cute when you're being completely irrational. He recognizes the "fact" that you are always right in every fight you get into with your mom. Essentially, you never even have to think about the way you're behaving, you don't even have to express your thoughts, and he always knows just what to say and do. Before we go any further, it's time for you to take a look at what makes up *your* Mr. Right.

THE PERFECT COUPLE?

There's no such thing as the "perfect relationship," but we are constantly exposed in books and movies to these mythical perfect relationships. Mostly, you get these ideas from modern-day romantic comedies in which the characters seem *so* real—the social worker living in New York, the wedding planner in San Francisco—why can't the relationship be real, too? Here are some of those couples:

- John Beckwith and Claire Cleary from *Wedding Crashers*
- Jonathan Trager and Sara Thomas in *Serendipity*
- Bridget Jones and Mark Darcy in *Bridget Jones' Diary*
- Andy Stitzer and Trish in *The 40-Year-Old Virgin*

Here is the thing. These characters, as real as they seem, have these perfect moments fall into their laps in which they suddenly realize "oh my God, we are a perfect match!" But, in real life, those hyper-revealing moments don't just fall into your lap. You have to do some work to pay attention and learn to identify if a man is kind, funny, intelligent, ambitious—whatever it is you're looking for—from more subtle, everyday events. And you need to make an effort to show a guy who you are because, odds are, he isn't just going to happen to catch you doing something that makes him realize you're the love of his life.

EXERCISE:
YOUR RELATIONSHIP EXPECTATIONS

In this exercise you will explore your desires and expectations for the man with whom you want a long-term relationship. You will begin to evaluate whether or not these expectations are reasonable. If you approach this exercise thinking there is nothing wrong with your expectations, you're not going to get anything out of it. Be open to the idea that you could be *wrong* sometimes.

1. Take out a piece of paper and write the words, "What I want from a rela-tionship" (or, if you're in a relationship write "What I want from [insert your guy's name here]") on the top of the page. Now, take five minutes and write everything that comes to mind. Some examples of what you want in a man could include:

    - Wants children
    - Handsome
    - Healthy
    - Faithful
    - Supportive
    - Good job
    - Rich
    - Sense of humor
    - Athletic
    - Intellectual

2. That was probably pretty easy, right? Now, for the harder part. When you take you need to give. Let's begin to explore what you are willing to bring to a relationship. At the top of the other side of the page, write "Within a relationship, I am willing to" and for the next five minutes, write down whatever you would be willing to give your partner in a romantic relation-ship. Some examples may include:

    - I'll be faithful
    - I'll give him good sex
    - I'll do most of the housework
    - I'll work and earn good money

- I'll keep myself attractive and thin
- I'll have one or more children
- I'll be good to his family
- I'll listen to him when he needs to vent about stress
- I'll make an effort to get to know his friends

3. Evaluate. Which of your lists is longer? Oftentimes when people have a hard time getting into good relationships, their expectations list is significantly longer than their giving list. This can happen for women in particular because we are conditioned to assume a man won't give us enough and to fight for whatever it is that *we* want. We are taught to state our needs, put our foot down, and not let men step all over us. Let's re-balance your views of giving and taking though by looking at your two lists. For a relationship to actually work, for each expectation you have for him, you should think about what you will give him in return. Not to say anyone should only be giving to receive, but there are certain expectations that need to match up in order for the relationship to run smoothly. You want him to listen to you vent? Maybe your promise should be to consider when it's actually worth it to complain so you don't end up taking advantage of his always listening ear. The idea is to meet at a midpoint in each particular dynamic of your relationship.

Now that you've created your list and see what you're looking for, take a good hard look at all of your requirements. Do you know anyone who could possibly live up to your expectations? Probably not. But do you know of some guys today who you would consider dating, or who you at least respect? Probably. Because while great relationships do exist in real life, guys as perfect as your ideal fictional character do not.

Dates can be stressful. For a more natural context, ask a guy to help you with a small task or project, such as the computer or buying a new car (make sure that you focus on a task at which he is skilled and put him in a situation in which he will be comfortable). Usually, he'll be happy to help. You can also just talk to him when the two of you are with a group of people. If he's interested in you, he will probably ask to spend time with you in private, but don't forget that you can always ask him too!

Soul Mate?

I hate to break it to you, but the idea of the soul mate, while romantic, is absurd. Think about it. The concept that there is just *one* Mr. Right out there searching for you seems just a little far-fetched, doesn't it? *One* person in the whole wide world? *One* person out of billions? No one is perfect; not you and not your partner. And expecting your guy to be perfect puts a lot of pressure on both him and your relationship. It's time to begin thinking more realistically about your relationships and take expectations like the following down a notch:

> **MYTH:** Once I meet my soul mate, all my needs will be fulfilled.
> **REALITY:** You cannot expect one person to fill all your needs.

You don't need a man for your life to be perfect. It's *your* job to make your life perfect. You don't need to be "saved" and you don't want to attract the type of guy who is looking to "save" someone. If you seem discontented with your life, and desperate to have someone fix it, you will attract men who see that in you and want to keep you down because it makes them feel good to be your "savior."

To attract men who want you to be happy, build the life you want to live alone. It may sound contradictory to the purpose of this book, but if you create a life that is based entirely on what makes you happy, then there is a better chance that when a guy does come in the picture, it will actually work out, because he gets to know the true you. He likes the version of you that *you* like too.

> **MYTH:** There is only one "Mr. Right" in the world for you.
> **REALITY:** Many men are your Mr. Right.

Many different things factor into your level of attraction for someone, including physical appearance, sense of humor, and intelligence. In fact, you could probably be attracted to many varieties within these traits.

And then of course there's chemistry. You know it when you feel it. But do you really know what's behind it? That term "chemistry" wasn't just applied to feelings of attraction because it's a cute term or phrase. There are actually dozens of biological processes that lead you to feel attracted to someone. Yup, there's science behind it—hence, chemistry. Recent biological research shows that you can be compatible with one out of eleven people. It has revealed to us that the feeling you associate with having found your soul mate is in fact a feeling you can and will have with *plenty* of people. That's kind of the opposite idea of a soul mate, isn't it?

Timing plays a huge role in who you date too. If you meet a man that seems terrific but who just got divorced or out of a serious relationship, he probably cannot give you the emotional connection you need—and you don't want to be a rebound. By the same token, don't look for a rebound. Don't desperately search for someone to distract you from the pain of a recent breakup. That relationship will be built from all the wrong materials. You'll most likely just look for someone who is *nothing* like your ex or *everything* like him. And that is not fair to the new guy because you won't look at him for who he is as an individual, but rather for how he matches up to the last guy. Your head and heart need to be substantially cleared of past relationships in order to clearly evaluate if a new one is any good.

> **MYTH:** If I feel a special bond with someone, that person must be my soul mate and the relationship is right for me.
> **REALITY:** Feeling a special bond with someone does not necessarily mean he's Mr. Right.

In fact, this guy may not even be right at all. You need to get over the idea that feeling a bond is indicative of a good match because this is the type of thing that can lead to outrageous behavior like spending hours going through every single person on Facebook or LinkedIn with his first name to see if you could find him. Odds are, even if you manage to track him down, that he's actually not someone you'd want to date in the first place.

DID YOU KNOW?

44 percent of the adult American population is single. That's over 100 million people, so your odds of finding someone are actually much better than you thought!

MYTH: Soul mates are destined to fit together, grow together, and live happily ever after.

REALITY: People do not grow at the same rate and expecting continual happiness is unrealistic.

To have continual happiness and harmony, you'd have to marry yourself. And if you want to do this, perhaps you should talk to a therapist about narcissism. We've all heard people say that when you're really in love, what's good for one person is good for the couple, but, that is just not always true. The reality is that you are two separate entities and, at times, your desires will conflict —especially as you grow older and you and your partner's interests change and mature. But if you know each other well enough and know what sorts of standards the other person holds for themselves, you can help them through those changes and vice versa. If you are two healthy, well-adjusted, and mature people involved in a healthy, well-adjusted, and mature relationship, then the changes life throws at you shouldn't shake you too much. Maybe at times you will waver a little and feel disconnected, but, if you are two healthy people who know what you want out of life, you will rediscover each other and feel close all over again.

The most important thing is that you find someone who can handle your problems and whose problems you can handle in return. Find someone who makes the real, even ugly sides of life easier. Yes, find someone who occasionally takes your breath away and makes you feel like you're living in a dream. But, for the most part, they need to be someone who makes right here, right now, bearable and even enjoyable. You find someone who is romantic? Hilarious? Brilliant? Interesting? Terrific. But what does he do when you throw a fit? What does he do when you cry? Or are stressed? He better be there then too and have good ways of coping with that. And you in turn should want to help him through his rough days.

SOUL MATE SCENARIOS:
Rita

Rita and Steve had been happily married for thirty years, and had two grown daughters. They did everything together, and seemed to fit like puzzle pieces: what Rita needed, Steve gave. He even enjoyed clothes shopping with Rita, waiting patiently outside her dressing room to comment on outfits and help her make decisions. Some women wouldn't think much of such a selfless act, but to Rita, it meant the world. It was just one of many reasons they believed they were soul mates.

But their deep connection wasn't enough to save them from tragedy. One night, Steve suffered a massive heart attack and passed away in his sleep. Rita was devastated. In the days that followed Steve's death, Rita became increasingly depressed. The life she'd envisioned with the person she loved ended abruptly. Her partner in everything was gone and where there had been someone meeting Rita's needs one day, there was emptiness the next.

After some time had passed, Rita's daughters placed an ad on a dating site under their mother's name. They wanted her to find *someone* to help fill the hole left by their father's death. After a few men responded, Rita agreed to try dating again, and it wasn't long before Rita met Craig. They had only been on a few dates before Rita admitted to her daughters that she felt a deep sense of closeness with Craig—one she hadn't felt with anyone before, except Steve. Craig even worked in the same industry Steve had, and the coincidence made Rita feel like this new relationship had been given her late husband's approval. As Rita grew closer to Craig, however, she discovered one problem: Craig hated to shop.

It may seem like a small problem, but Rita had spent years deeply in love with a man who met *every* need she had. She'd grown deeply accustomed to seeing Steve's love of shopping as love for her as well, so when Craig admitted that he didn't like to shop, it felt as though he'd told Rita he didn't love her.

Rita's story isn't so unusual. Think of a time when someone you cared for—whether it was a family member, a friend, or a boyfriend—admitted that something you loved deeply wasn't something that person appreciated. Perhaps your were offended and maybe you even ended the relationship over it. But, your partner isn't your clone. And, that's a good thing. After all, even if you think you're great, do you really want to date yourself? That would get boring pretty fast. So, instead, if you find your partner—or your next partner—doesn't have the same interests or level of interest in something as you do, find someone (a friend, a group, etc.) to fill that need of yours.

In the end, Rita and Craig didn't break up over shopping. She found a friend to accompany her on shopping trips. Because she was able to separate her unfulfilled needs from her love for Craig, Rita strengthened her relationship, her friendship, and *herself.*

LESSON: Rely on yourself and *all* of the people you love to find happiness, not just one person!

Stop Holding Out

Believing that one single soul mate is going to come in and share all your interests and make you completely, blissfully happy is not only ridiculous, it can also strip you of your power. No man is going to waltz into your life and put on a show to display all of his colors without you doing any work. It just isn't going to happen. And if it seems like it does, and you meet a guy you think is perfect immediately, just know that first impressions actually mean *nothing*. Instead of just sitting and waiting for someone perfect to fall into your life, do some ground work. Get out there and get to know someone. See a guy in multiple settings so that all of his colors have a chance to come out.

Historical Soul Mates

It's important for you to know that you're not the only one holding out for something "perfect." In Rutgers University's 2001 National Marriage Project Survey, 94 percent of twenty- to twenty-nine-year-olds agreed with the statement: "When you marry, you want your spouse to be your soul mate, first and foremost." Another 88 percent agreed that: "There is a special person, a soul mate, waiting for you out there." But this isn't just some modern trend: the idea that soul mates exist has been around for ages.

But where does the term "soul mate" even come from in the first place? Well, Plato theorized that humans originally had four arms and four legs. These beings were capable of toppling the Gods if they desired, so the Gods split their bodies—and their souls—in half. According to this Greek philosopher, we're doomed to spend our lives searching for our other half: our soul's mate.

People who believe in reincarnation feel that your soul mate is someone you knew in a past life that you have unfinished business to complete together in this lifetime. But no matter how you came across the concept, one thing is true: there isn't one perfect man who is going to make your life perfect. The good news is that truth doesn't have to be buried under a lifetime of wrong turns: the basics are all right here.

So What Should You Expect?

As we progress, we'll talk about what are reasonable expectations to have in a healthy relationship and what are unreasonable expectations. And, we'll address the areas in which you might not be holding up your end of the bargain and how you can improve. But before we get that far let's take a look at the following chart that lays out some realistic and unrealistic expectations. How do your expectations line up?

REASONABLE	UNREASONABLE
My partner should be faithful to me.	My partner should not speak with other women.
My partner should care about my needs.	My partner should anticipate all of my needs.
My partner should meet many of my needs.	My partner should meet all of my needs.
My partner should be attractive to me.	My partner must be handsome.
My partner should have a good work ethic.	My partner should earn six figures.
I should enjoy activities with my partner.	My partner must enjoy everything that I enjoy.
I expect to work hard if I want a loving relationship.	If we love one another, we'll live happily ever after.
My partner and I should fight fair.	My partner and I should never fight.
My partner should understand my culture and religion.	My partner must be of the same culture and religion.
My partner and I should have some separate friends and interests.	My partner and I must do everything together.

You'll notice some pretty unreasonable or irrational expectations on the table that many women often don't realize they have. And, in fact, it's easy to step over the line from rational to irrational without realizing it. Hopefully, when you take a look at the two corresponding expectations lined up next to one another, you can actually see which one you have and whether or not it is reasonable. But, naturally, for someone to be a suitable partner for you, they *do* have to meet certain requirements. Just keep in mind these requirements should be created by *you*. They should be what *you're* comfortable with.

For instance, let's say your closest friends are interested in dating wealthy men and they've told you that you should try and date older, wealthier men so you can enjoy the creature comforts that could come with that lifestyle. But, creativity and emotional stability are more important to you than wealth. And, as a result, you tend to date sweet, creative types who struggle financially. That's okay! It's important to be true to yourself. Of course not all creative types struggle financially and not all wealthy men are emotionally unstable. But you need to identify what quality it is that you like within a man and look for that, rather than exterior traits that your girlfriends suggest you look for. Read on to find out how to make sure you're picking characteristics that matter.

DID YOU KNOW?

According to a recent study done in the UK, the average woman will date twenty-four men and spend more than $3,200 on fancy clothes, singles vacations, online and in-person dating services, club memberships, bars, and social events before she finds the man she'll marry. So before you settle for a "soul mate," make sure you're getting what you paid for: real compatibility.

The Real Points of Compatibility

To determine more important points of compatibility you must be willing to take a close look at a guy you're interested in. For example, pay close attention to things like the following:

- How does he treat his family and friends?
- How did his prior relationship end?
- If he has children, is he very involved with them?

It may sound old fashioned, but it's true; the way he treats others is the way he is likely to treat you. This is because past behavior is the best predictor of future behavior. Many women fall into the trap of dating a man because they see potential in him to change. But you know what? You don't want to be constantly goading someone to change when there's a man out there who is already closer to being a good match for you.

As tempting as it might be to pick a partner who shares the same entertainment choices, political affiliations, religion, etc., those factors aren't enough to guarantee a happy, long-lasting relationship. Instead of searching for someone who shares your love of Thai food and '80s movies, you'll be much closer to finding a great lifelong companion if you look for someone who lines up with you on the following characteristics.

Respect

What does respect mean to you? Does it mean not interrupting you? Does it mean asking you before he plans something for the two of you? Does it mean listening to your requests and delivering on them? And, if so, how many of them? Respect is important in a relationship—and it needs to come from both of you—but make sure your expectations aren't so high that you're setting up the other person for failure. Respect does *not* mean that a man should never, ever argue with you if you are the one being irrational. Respect means that you both care enough about one another to offer constructive criticism, as well as kind, supportive words.

Trust

If you even have to wonder whether you're likely to catch your partner in constant lies—or vice versa—your relationship does not have much of a future. You have to be able to trust the person you're with. Otherwise your relationship doesn't stand a chance of lasting for the long term. Some couples are very good at lying and become addicted to the game of catching the other one in a lie as well as sneaking things past the other one. Usually these will be people with immense pride who can't learn to walk away from an unhealthy relationship. But this type of relationship becomes more of a competition than a connection. No real intimacy can be achieved without honesty.

Fidelity

Is emotional or physical fidelity more important to you? Are they equally important? Are you capable yourself of monogamy? If you desire a long-term, monogamous relationship, in what ways would you and your partner work to continue to fulfill each other sexually? These are all important questions to ask of both yourself and your partner. Some people believe in traditional monogamy while others are okay with the lines being more blurred. Neither is right or wrong, but this is one area where you want to make sure that the two of you agree.

SOUL MATE SCENARIOS:
Alicia

Joe and Alicia had been married ten years and had two beautiful daughters, ages three and eight. Alicia had always had difficulties accepting Joe's "kinky" sexual preferences for things like bondage, spanking, and the use of sex toys. But in spite of her reservations, Alicia tried to accommodate Joe. She had grown up in a family where she was aware that her mother often rejected her father's advances. As a result, Alicia's father became cold, rejecting, and abusive towards his wife and children. He eventually left her mother for another woman. Alicia did not want to lose Joe's affection by putting demands on their sex life so she tolerated what she considered to be greater and greater aberrations from traditional love and sex. When she refused Joe's request to go to a sex club, he began an affair. Later she found out that he had already had several affairs, in spite of the fact that she usually accommodated his sexual requests.

Knowing that she eventually wanted to leave this relationship, Alicia went back to work as a teacher and soon she met Frank, who was in the middle of a divorce. They became friendly; and when his divorce was final, Frank asked Alicia to go out for dinner. While she felt guilty, Alicia agreed to go on the date.

Eventually Alicia and Frank fell in love. They shared much in common: they were both teachers and they both had relatively conservative values regarding marital fidelity and sexual desires. Alicia ended up divorcing Joe and, soon after, she and Frank wed.

Eventually, Alicia felt comfortable opening up to Frank about the issues she had had with Joe. Frank expressed amazement that Alicia had tolerated Joe's request for alternate sexual activities throughout the years of their marriage. Alicia then realized that it was Joe, and not herself, who had excessive demands. Today, aside from the usual arguments that accompany a long-term relationship, Alicia and Frank are very happy together, due in no small part to their similar values and morals when it comes to what's acceptable and unacceptable in their relationship.

LESSON: Alicia and Joe obviously had very serious differences regarding sexual activity, faithfulness, and deal-breakers. But when someone believes in the idea of the soul mate, and they believe their current partner is that soul mate, they often force themselves to do things they are uncomfortable with, with the reasoning that "my soul mate wouldn't ask me to do anything that was bad for me." In reality, there is no such thing as a soul mate and you could just be two different people with different preferences that don't work well together.

The concept of monogany is constantly being redefined. Today, some couples go to swinger's parties, have threesomes, and even encourage one another to have an affair in order to keep the excitement alive in their partnership. None of these practices are right or wrong and you and your partner should feel free to explore new methods of keeping your relationship exciting. What is wrong, however, is forcing your partner to try anything that they do not agree with. That will not only not benefit the relationship, but may actually hurt it.

Companionship

Different people have different needs for companionship. Some people like to tell their partner everything. Others prefer to have more independent individual lives. It's important that you and your partner are on the same page as far as companionship is concerned. It can be an extremely lonely feeling to be in a relationship with someone who wants to share *less* with you than you want to share with them. On the flip side, it can feel overwhelming to be in a relationship in which your partner wants you involved in very part of his life while you like to keep many aspects of your life separate from your relationship. A good way to determine what type of companionship a guy will want is to observe his parents. Are they the type of couple who is best friends—who are together constantly, who update each other on every detail from their lives and always seem to be on the same page? Or do they lead more separate lives, only spending a few hours a day together and generally out of touch with what is going on in the other one's life? It's kind of the typical psychologist way to view it, but your parents *do* play a large role in the formation of your opinions and your partner's parents' relationship can be a good indicator of what sort of relationship he wants. That being said, people can be self-reflective. Your partner may want to be *nothing* like this parents. Pay attention to how he speaks of their relationship—does he admire it, or does he want to veer away from that type of relationship? You have to talk about it to find out.

Affection

To have a good relationship, there has to be sexual attraction and, in addition, there should also be loving gestures between the two of you. There are four main ways you and your partner can communicate affection for each other:

- **Verbal:** where you tell your partner the ways in which you love him

- **Tactile:** where you touch each other in loving ways
- **Sexual:** where you touch your partner in ways that will give him physical pleasure
- **Demonstrative:** where you do things for your partner that are loving. This could be preparing dinner for him, buying him a gift he had been eyeing in a store, or doing other things that make his personal life as an individual easier and more enjoyable.

Different people respond more to different types of affection. The type of affection people respond to depends upon multiple factors. These include your family history, memories of prior relationships, myths, and realities that both of you have been exposed to throughout your lifetime. For instance, you might like to hear your partner say he loves you, but to him, the little gestures you do for him are more important. But even if you and your partner express your affection in different ways, in order to have a healthy, long-lasting relationship, it must absolutely be expressed.

Some couples can get so caught up in the dynamic of making fun of one another (lovingly, of course) that they become uncomfortable exchanging pure, straightforward compliments or affectionate words. While it's great to be able to joke around with each other and point out one another's flaws in a light manner, if you still want to feel comfortable being vulnerable in front of your partner—which is so important in a relationship—then you have to keep the pure affection up as well.

The final condition is that you both *understand* in what ways the other shows affection. So many couples fight because they don't think the other is showing enough affection, but they simply don't recognize how their partner shows affection. For example, you might feel unloved because your partner doesn't show you much physical affection in public, but you don't recognize the ways he tries to show you that love in contexts in which he is more comfortable, like by making you dinner or even being extremely generous in bed.

Conflict

Couples fight. Spend enough time with anyone and you're bound to have a skirmish or two. And while ideally you shouldn't be fighting often, in the long run, how you fight is more important than what you fight about. To avoid feeling like your partner has turned into a completely different person when you get into an argument, observe the way he fights with his family. Are they yellers? Even name-callers? Or do they sit down and have a calm discussion? Are they passive, ignoring the issue altogether? If you find this out ahead of time, you shouldn't be surprised if your partner displays traits that you had never seen in him before, such as yelling or passiveness. If you and your partner do have different fighting styles, it is going to take a lot of effort to be conscious of that when you are in a fight. It's easy to feel that your partner overreacts to things or doesn't care enough about an issue simply because you do not understand their style of fighting. It's tough, but you'll have to remind yourself that their style of fighting is not necessarily an indicator of how much they care about you or the issue at hand, because on top of fighting about the original issue, you don't want to get into yet another fight about how you both deal with issues.

Similar Values and Goals

These include basic attitudes towards family, children, sex, money, and religion or spirituality. If the two of you differ in some of these attitudes, you should at least agree on how to navigate that difference. Essential differences can include such issues as one person wanting many children, while the other person wants none. One person spends every weekend with their parents; and the other person sees their parents every six months.

One person wants sex every day; another person wants sex once a month. While these differences are not insurmountable barriers to a good relationship, they must be considered seriously—along with solutions and compromises—before a long-term commitment is made. It's easy to ignore these differences in the beginning of a relationship because you are excited and you think that your feelings for one another will magically make those problems become a nonissue, but you will eventually have to face those issues if you get serious with this person. To avoid heartache and strife later—which, in case you've forgotten, is the reason you're reading this—address these differences as you see them occur in the beginning of the relationship. That way you will get an idea of whether or not you can work through them.

SOUL MATE SCENARIOS:
Mary Ann

Most people have some amount of unreasonable expectations, but expecting too much from your partner doesn't bode well for a long-term relationship. How much is too much? Let's look at Mary Ann's story to get an idea.

Mary Ann was raised in a very prim and proper family where her family members never expressed their negative emotions. As a result, she grew up without the knowledge of how to do so in an appropriate way and kept her emotions bottled up inside of her. She also had a very low tolerance for anyone who seemed to be breaking what her idea was of the social norm. Since she had trained herself to stifle her emotions in order to make others comfortable, she thought it was inconsiderate when someone else just laid their emotions out for everyone to see and deal with.

When she was in her early twenties, Mary Ann began dating Mike, an investment banker and gentleman. He usually asked for Mary Ann's approval before he did anything—even go out with his friends—and he kept his opinions to himself if he felt they would upset her. Eventually, the pair started to think about getting engaged.

But one day, Mary Ann, Mike, and Mike's little sister were playing a card game and there arose a dispute between her and the younger sister regarding whose move was right. Mike made a call in favor of his sister and jokingly said, "Blood is thicker than water." Mary Ann was appalled he chose his sister's side over her own and even more by his willingness to outwardly admit he was choosing a side—that is, acknowledging conflict. She hardly said a word to him for the rest of the day, and later that evening told him she had to rethink their relationship.

It's easy to see that her very low tolerance for conflict or for anyone disagreeing with her was unreasonable and was likely to cause anyone she dated to bottle up their feelings and lash out from time to time. To get over an argument, both partners need to be open to the idea that they could be the one at fault. Mary Ann was so resistant to the idea that perhaps Mike's sister was correct that she ended up becoming irrationally upset with Mike for siding with his sister. And Mike's harsh words clearly showed some pent up resentment he had towards Mary Ann for her need to always be agreed with. But in a healthy relationship, each partner should feel comfortable expressing his or her honest opinion and disagreeing with the other, without fearing that this will cause tension. Mike came to a therapy session with Mary Ann and the two of them learned how to express differing opinions in constructive ways. The two of them are still together today.

LESSON: It's important to be understanding of your partner and of yourself. Conflict is okay, but try to see the other as an ally—not an enemy. Remember that if he loves you, he is not arguing with you for the sake of arguing. He simply feels comfortable expressing his opinion, even when it differs from yours.

Bending, Not Breaking

The bad news is that even your best match is going to disappoint you from time to time. After all, he's only human and he can't live inside of your head to know your every desire. And even if he did, wouldn't you prefer that he had a mind of his own and acted on that rather than walking on eggshells for you? However, it can be so disappointing when a man who a woman thought was perfect for her disappoints her, that she calls off the relationship all together, when that really wasn't necessary. This will especially happen if you buy into the myth of the soul mate, because disappointment and turbulence don't exist in that fairy tale. But, don't get too dramatic. Just because your straight, seamless relationship bends a little doesn't mean it has to break.

A good relationship consists of bad times, as well as good times. The test of a long-term relationship is whether you've overcome hardships such as disagreements, illness, finances, children, and other stressful experiences. Some ways to maintain this attitude include the following:

Accept Differences

If your partner were your clone your relationship would probably be awfully dull. Luckily, you and your partner aren't exactly the same, but at times this means that he's going to do things that rub you the wrong way and some of those things aren't going to change over time. The more you can accept him for who he is and realize he doesn't do things intentionally to annoy or disappoint you (and the more he can accept you for who you are), the happier you will be with him and with the relationship.

Appreciate Him

Want to encourage more of those affectionate feelings between you and your partner? Show him how much you appreciate what he *does* do. Sometimes, you may get into a bad habit of taking your partner for granted and while you may be quick to point out their flaws, you're likely not as speedy to thank him and tell him how he makes you feel special when he's doing things you like. It's easy to get into the mindset of constantly looking for flaws, especially after a guy's done something wrong. In an effort to protect yourself from being walked all over, you may develop the tactic of being always on the defense and on the lookout for ways a man mistreats you, meanwhile becoming blind to the ways he treats you well. You know those guys who roll their eyes and silence their phones when their girlfriend is calling? You don't want to be that girlfriend. Don't make your partner afraid that every time you open your mouth you're going to criticize him, because then he will just tiptoe around you, giving you false affection in the ways he *thinks* you want it. Keep your eyes out for the *good* things he does for you and let him know you see them. Positive reinforcement will get you a lot further —and make you a lot happier—in a relationship than negative reinforcement ever will.

Don't Play Mind Games

Have you ever stared at your partner and tried to beam your thoughts into his head hoping he'll just "get it"? Here's a little inside knowledge for you: One, your attempts at telepathy aren't working. Two, if he catches you staring at him, he'll think you're either angry with him or obsessively imagining your future marriage and your perfect life. If you are discontent with something, express it. Which brings us to our next point. . . .

Pick Your Battles

We've already discussed that it's unrealistic to expect that your partner will have all the same priorities, manners, and interests as you. And if you start fights over every little thing, your partner will start to believe that no matter what he does it'll never be enough and even the best relationship will fall apart. A man will not stay in a relationship if he does not believe he can make you happy. All this type of a relationship does is exhaust him and kill his ego. So, before you engage him in a discussion—or worse, start accusing him—about what he is or isn't doing, make sure it's something that is still going to matter in ten years. Or ten days.

Short and Sweet Is Best

Most guys dread having any sort of "talk." Why? Because many women can discuss emotional issues *forever*. Of course, it doesn't feel like forever to us, but to them, it's as though they're watching their lives slowly melt away before them. And, the longer the talk goes on, the more likely it is that they'll just say anything they can to get out of it. "Sorry" is a golden little word men keep in their pocket for any time you get angry with them. And they will pull it out even if they have no idea what they did wrong *or* if they don't even think they did anything wrong. When a guy has a problem with another guy, they usually don't sit down over coffee and talk it out for hours. Instead, one guy will usually just say to the other something akin to, "Dude, what you did was not cool. Don't do it again." The other guy responds with, "Okay." Point made, end of discussion. Granted, some issues are bigger than this and you want more discussion just so you can be certain your man *actually* understands what he did wrong and how to remedy it or change that behavior in the future. But, if you feel you need to have a discussion with your man that can't be summarized in a few sentences, there are a few things to keep in mind.

To start off, don't bring the issue up at a moment when you clearly don't even have the time to have that discussion. If he is rushing to gather things up and run out the door for a meeting, don't casually drop the fact that you wish he'd stand up to his mother more, or whatever the issue might be. Also, tone is everything. Some women give a man a critique, but they say it in a way that seems they don't even believe the man is capable of changing it. Make it clear that you are open to discussion, and you don't just want to talk at him. A good way to do this is look him in the eyes when you tell him what's bothering you. This seems like a no-brainer, but women can become passive when bringing up an issue and it makes it seem to him that you don't actually care to hear what he has to say. Bring up the issue as more of a question than a statement. Pose it in a way that shows you're open to hearing an explanation. He'll appreciate that you want to understand where he's coming from and in turn, you'll get what you want, which is a discussion.

Once you've stated your desires clearly, step back and see what happens. If he takes them into consideration and makes an honest attempt to adjust his behavior, praise him for doing so. He might not get it right the first time, or the second, or even the third, but if you continue to make him feel appreciated for whatever strides he is making, he'll be more likely to continue to head in the direction you want because he won't feel like he's being forced to do so. That said, if you find your self constantly having to let your man know that he's behaving in a way that is not in your best interest, this relationship might not be the best one for you.

PROGRESS REPORT

How are your expectations doing? Are you terrified of the changes you have to make? Or did you already know all of this? Here's a handy checklist to see if you're on track. Take a look at the following items and consider how you feel about each. What do you expect your partner to do in each situation? Note: Not all items will be applicable to your life, but it's time to do a quick check-in.

- Your partner wants you to hang out with him and his friends more often.
- You can have fun doing something on your own while he participates in an activity and without feeling like you need to check in on him.
- You enjoy attending services at his place of worship.
- He quits a well-paid job for moral reasons and you feel happy for him.
- You and your partner can agree to disagree on certain issues without lingering bad feelings.
- You feel good about yourself when you're both with and without him (or if you're single!).

Soul Mate Summary

Finding Mr. Right and having a good relationship is all about having reasonable expectations—both for yourself and for your partner. Perhaps in the past you've been overly demanding of your partner, or wanted more than he was willing to give. But you deserve more—and so does he! As you move forward, keep the following in mind:

- There are reasonable and unreasonable expectations in a relationship, and sometimes the line is very fine between them. Certain qualities such as respect, fidelity, affection, and compatibility are reasonable to expect from a partner in a long-term relationship. Other expectations that include specific requirements as well as expectations that one's partner will meet each and every one of your needs, or have exactly the same interests, are unreasonable expectations for a partner.

- All relationships require effort. Both of you must work on the relationship. If it appears that one is not doing his or her share, this must be addressed and resolved to maintain the balance in the relationship.

- For a relationship to succeed and grow, both partners, as individuals and together, must regularly look at ways that they can improve themselves and the relationship. You cannot expect a man to fix your life. You are responsible for making yourself happy in the areas of your life outside of the relationship.

- In a good relationship there is a balanced distribution of responsibilities. From time to time, each of you should adjust what your responsibilities are and look towards maintaining a fair balance.

- There is no such thing as a perfect man.

- The idea of one and only one soul mate is baloney. There are endless combinations of personality types, senses of humor, physical attributes, and intelligences that will add up to a good match for you.

- You need to be happy on your own before you can be happy in a relationship.

As we progress, you'll learn about what fears are preventing you from having fulfilling relationships, how to adjust your expectations so they're more realistic, and how to tell what is real love and what isn't. But, first, let's travel over to the science lab to see what's going on behind the scenes.

CHAPTER 2

Your Brain on Love

Like it or not, chemistry plays a role—a large one, in fact—in whom you fall in love with. The word chemistry gets thrown around a lot. The general understanding of it is the feeling that is created when two people are together. But chemistry—even when it applies to relationships—actually has to do with your brain. Yes, you're a smart and observant woman. You know that certain traits are good and you look for those in a man. So you must be in control of who you fall for, right? Sort of. But it's the actual chemistry in your brain that made you search for those traits in the first place.

While you're busy swooning, there's a lot going on behind the scenes. There are years of evolutionary biology playing out and your genes are actually telling you who would make a great match—and who wouldn't. As you read through this chapter, don't get discouraged and start to feel like the love you've experienced before—or are possibly experiencing now—wasn't "real." Your feelings *are* real. They just might be coming from a different place than you thought.

Studying Love

Since you now know that love is essentially chemistry, you must be dying to find out the formula. Gym membership + Match.com membership = Lifelong love. Unfortunately, it's not that simple. However, over the years, physicians, scientists and psychologists have dived deep enough into the subject to come back with some answers.

In 1890, English physician Dr. Havelock Ellis proposed one of the first love "formulas," which read simply: Love = Sex + Friendship. As simple as this sounds, this was one of the first attempts to define love in scientific terms. And, it makes sense if you think about it. Have you ever had one of those hot, passionate flings where you barely leave the bedroom for days but once you do, and you're sitting in the light of day, or standing agitated in line at Starbucks, you realize the two of you have nothing to talk about. He doesn't bring anything to your life outside of the bedroom. And, as it just so happens, most people spend the vast majority of their lives outside of the bedroom, so, it would be nice to be with someone who makes that time enjoyable, too. In fact, for couples who have enjoyed long, happy relationships, their romantic partner is not only someone they're attracted to, that partner is often also one of their best friends.

Thirty-three years after Ellis created his formula, the famed psychiatrist Carl Jung proposed a theory within his book *Modern Man in Search of a Soul* that described love as a chemical reaction. He wrote, "The meeting of two personalities is like the contact of two chemical substances; if there is any reaction, both are transformed." Jung focused mostly on unconscious human processes, as opposed to the hard sciences of chemistry and biology, and meant this chemical comparison as an analogy, however, he was more right than anyone would have thought.

These early attempts at trying to define love in more scientific terms—terms that were quantifiable and, thus, able to be studied—laid the groundwork for the truly groundbreaking research that would come decades later. Within the past fifteen years, significant advances have been made in the field of science, ones that have enabled medical practitioners to perform brain scans, study how emotions affect our internal processes, and figure out how hormones and neurotransmitters work together to help us find lasting love—or, how these might actually be getting in the way. But before you know how your chemistry works, you need to know what you're dealing with, so read on.

SINGLE LADIES

Have you ever met a man who just made you hot, where the chemistry is there from the get go? You don't want to come on as someone who's too desperate or too pushy but you don't want to let this wonderful man slip away either. Here are a few ideas that will help you get what you want:

- **Make the first move:** Don't be afraid to go after what—and who—you want. Odds are, if there really is chemistry, it will feel pretty effortless to talk to him.
- **Be confident:** If you act like you're a catch, he's going to be intrigued. Take confidence in the fact that chemistry pretty much only arises when two people are being themselves because chemistry is not something you can control or manipulate.
- **Flatter him:** You might be afraid to do this but, sitting in the corner alone is a 100 percent guarantee you won't meet someone.

Hormones

When you experience lust, have sex, or decide you're ready for a long-term commitment, your body is busy releasing hormones, the chemicals released by a cell or gland in one part of the body, that act as signals or catalysts for change in another part of the body. Each stage of love, from attraction to romance to attachment, has its own set of hormones that are activated. You know how a breakup can cause pain that seems beyond your control? No matter how many funny movies you watch or bottles of wine you drink, you cannot reason or distract yourself out of that pain? That's because reason isn't everything when it comes to feeling attached to someone. Hormones can make the breakup process a painful, drawn-out one. However, something else they can do is make you feel attracted to a man that will make you a good match. That being said, when you meet a guy that you feel immense chemistry with it's important to keep in mind that the forces of the universe haven't conspired to make sure you meet this one man at this one place and time. Instead, your hormones are simply responding to stimuli that you could have found in a whole slew of men. Each hormone your body produces does something different so keep reading to learn more about the relationship between specific hormones and love.

Testosterone

Though it's present in the female body, testosterone is *the* male hormone responsible for aggression and sex drive. Younger women are attracted to men with higher testosterone levels during their high fertility years. This attraction comes from an evolutionary place. Back in the day, men with higher testosterone levels were not only more likely to impregnate women, but they could protect them from predators, and were able to perform work requiring much physical ability. However, testosterone levels increase as women get older; and decrease as men advance in age. This explains why the sexes exhibit more similar personality characteristics as they get older. Women often become more confident and aggressive as their testosterone levels increase; while men become less aggressive and more likely to maintain long-term attachment, once their youthful high-testosterone playboy stage has come to an end.

Estrogen

Estrogen increases your sex drive as well as your vaginal secretions, which contain pheromones, those chemicals produced by animals and humans that give off sexual and aggressive messages to members of the same species. When women ovulate their bodies produce extremely high levels of estrogen because the female body is programmed to be more attractive and more sexual during the period when fertility levels are at their peak. In general, high estrogen women tend to be attracted to high-testosterone men. The feminine women want protection of a man who appears to be high in masculine traits, such as height, muscle, and body hair. In today's world, you probably have enough of an income to provide for your child (if you have one) and you live in an environment where you aren't constantly fighting off wild animals. However, humans evolved in a more hostile environment where food was scarce and predators were everywhere, so to that prehistoric woman lurking inside of you, a man with high testosterone levels is able to impregnate you and protect you and your offspring. As women approach menopause, estrogen levels drop significantly as fertility decreases, but they can be prematurely decreased by poor diet, lack of exercise, or abuse of alcohol and drugs.

THE ESTROGEN QUIZ

The following quiz will give you an idea of where your estrogen levels fall. Hormone levels play a part in determining who you are attracted to, another piece of evidence against the soul mate myth. You may have thought you wanted a "man's man" but your quiz results might actually show that you fit better with a man with lower testosterone levels. You may have thought you wanted you and your partner to be equals when it came to responsibilities in a relationship, but your results might show you that in reality, you want to be treated like a *woman;* you want to be taken care of and fill a more traditionally female role. To find out if your estrogen levels are high, medium, or low answer the following questions with the most appropriate answer.

1. You are most attracted to:
   a. Ryan Gosling
   b. Jude Law
   c. Ewan McGregor

2. You have your eye on an expensive ring. To encourage your partner to get it for you, do you:
   a. point it out in the store window
   b. wear your sexiest outfit so you know you'll have his full attention when you tell him about the one you saw
   c. wait until he asks you what you want for your birthday and tell him

3. As a woman you identify most with:
   a. Hillary Clinton
   b. Marilyn Monroe
   c. Lady Gaga

4. Your favorite outfit for going out at night is:
   a. an A-line skirt
   b. a fancy dress
   c. a simple cocktail dress

5. As a woman you'd most like to step into the shoes of:
   a. Jillian Michaels
   b. Brooklyn Decker
   c. Zooey Deschanel

6. Your favorite pastime is:
   a. hiking
   b. shopping
   c. reading

7. For a date you would choose:
   a. miniature golf
   b. dinner at an expensive restaurant
   c. a popular movie

8. Your ideal number of children is:
   a. zero or one
   b. the more the better
   c. two or three

9. To look sexy you wear:
   a. long tight skirt
   b. a top with a plunging neckline
   c. a short skirt

10. Your manicure is:
   a. clean, no polish
   b. long fingernails, colored polish
   c. medium fingernails, light polish

Scoring

Give your self one point for every a, three points for every b, and two points for every c. Add the total.

Scores

If you scored 10 to 16, you are likely to be a woman with low estrogen levels. You likely see men as equal partners. If you scored 17 to 23, you are likely a woman with medium estrogen levels. You likely want men to be dominant in the sense of doing the more demanding tasks and being gentlemen, but otherwise you'd prefer to be on equal footing. If you scored 24 to 30, you are likely a woman with high estrogen levels who prefers traditional roles for men and women.

Of course, you're welcome to go with these or against these as they're broad generalizations, but think about your history for a moment and see where your boyfriends have fit in. Are you more true to your chemical type than you thought?

USE YOUR PHEROMONES TO YOUR ADVANTAGE

The truth is, attraction is usually sexual before it evolves into emotional or mental attraction. Try going out on the town around the time when you're ovulating. Studies have shown that women release more pheromones during that time. In a study performed by J. Richard Udry at the University of North Carolina, women were rated as sexier during ovulation. Because while humans do not have such an acute sense of smell as animals, pheromones can be sensed unconsciously by the male human "animal," who is, in turn, more likely to be attracted to a woman "in heat." So when your hormones are acting up, take advantage of it and put your body's chemistry to good use!

Progesterone

Do you ever just feel asexual? You're not getting hit on much and you don't even care? You could just be producing progesterone. This hormone, most present in your blood post-ovulation, is sometimes described as the "Not Tonight" hormone. That's because it lowers your sex drive in preparation for possible pregnancy. It's also the time of the month when you're least likely to fall in love and be sexually enticing to others, making it a great time to schedule girls' nights in. Don't worry, you'll be back to your lustful, flirtatious self in no time.

Dehydroepiandrosterone (DHEA)

Similar to estrogen, this hormone increases your sex drive and is released just prior to ovulation. It is abundant during orgasm and creates an overall feeling of well-being. It is the biological reason that explains why you have an extra strut in your step the day after great sex. Unfortunately, this contentment-bringing hormone decreases as you reach menopause, but if you find yourself dragging, DHEA supplements can ease pre-menopausal or menopausal symptoms.

Norepinepherine

You know the butterflies in your stomach and the rose-colored glasses you wear at the beginning of a relationship? That's the excitement chemical norepinephrine taking hold. This hormone is responsible for increased energy, passion, and a strong sex drive in new relationships. Just because those feelings subside doesn't mean the guy isn't right for you. You can reignite that honeymoon feeling in a longer-term relationship. It can be kick-started by participating in interesting, exciting activities with your significant other.

BUST OUT OF THAT BOX!

You don't have to label yourself as totally "girly" or more of a "guy's girl." A number of factors can determine how much you fill the typical female gender role and it is okay to waver. Be with someone who understands that even though you may be an even-tempered person most of the time, sometimes you get emotional and act like more of a stereotypical female. Or, if you are someone who generally does fulfill the typical gender role, feel free to be with someone who won't freak out if you do feel like being more dominant on certain days. You don't *have* to fit into any role. And your partner shouldn't force you into one.

Oxytocin

When you experience loving physical contact—either romantic *or* platonic—your body releases oxytocin. Sometimes referred to as the "cuddle chemical," it helps stimulate long-term attachment after a couple passes through the initial passion phase. Massaging, snuggling, and other intimate activities increase oxytocin levels in the body, but these levels rise significantly during kissing and foreplay and peak at orgasm. So keep the effects of this hormone in mind if you have a one-night stand or a lingering casual sex relationship with someone. You don't want to confuse how this hormone is making you feel with actual love!

THE DANGERS OF ORGASMS

As bizarre—and backwards!—as it might sound, a recent study suggests that your orgasms can affect your love life in a negative way. During orgasm, fear and anxiety levels go down, and levels of dopamine in the blood go up, making you more relaxed. Unfortunately following orgasm, dopamine levels fall, which can produce a mild feeling of depression. Have you ever noticed you can feel sad after sex? So, what's the solution? Enjoy the big O but make sure you follow it with some cuddling to get your dopamine and oxytocin levels humming again.

Vasopressin

Women have been trained to believe that we feel more than men do—that we get more attached and feel love stronger than they do. Not true. Vasopressin, the "commitment" chemical, is responsible for creating loving memories and passionate thoughts during sexual intercourse. Vasopressin is also viewed as the male counterpart of the female hormone oxytocin and men who have lower levels of testosterone and/or are in long-term, committed relationships tend to have high levels of this hormone. Women have more oxytocin, to balance out the fact that men have both chemicals.

Neurotransmitters

Hormones aren't the only molecules that affect your love life. Neurotransmitters—chemicals, which transmit signals from one neuron to the next, across connective tissues or synapses—are similar to hormones, but instead of being released by glands, they're released by your neurons, the cells of the nervous system that are specialized to carry information by electrical and chemical signaling to other neurons. The most important neurotransmitters affecting love are the following.

Endorphins

Within the body, endorphins relieve pain and produce an overall feeling of well-being. In love, they are thought to be the primary hormone that causes attachment within long-term relationships. Like oxytocin, endorphin levels increase in response to touch, pleasing visual stimuli (such as a smile), or after having positive thoughts about your lover.

Phenylethylamine (PEA): The Risk-Taking Chemical

This amphetamine-like molecule speeds up the flow of information between nerve cells and keeps you alert, confident, and ready to try something new. It also produces an overall feeling of anticipation and well-being, which can lead you to experiment and enjoy the excitement of a new romantic partner.

Dopamine: The Passion Chemical

Dopamine is known as the "desire neurotransmitter" and is high during the initial phases of attraction and passionate romance. The brain tells the body to produce dopamine through the following process: Your eyes see a person who appears attractive to you. Your optic nerve relays the information to your brain, instructing the brain to produce dopamine. This chemical energizes and motivates you to approach the object of your attraction —which is just what you need if you're nervous about going up to a guy. Dopamine is also associated with increased energy and aggression, which can give you the extra boost of motivation and confidence that you may need to put yourself out there.

DID YOU KNOW?

London neuroscientists discovered that when a woman looks *directly* at a man who finds her attractive, she floods his brain with dopamine.

Serotonin: The Stability Chemical

High serotonin levels are associated with overall feelings of calm, comfort, and well-being. The relationship of these chemicals to one's feelings of love are important because this explains why one experiences romantic feelings towards their partner in different degrees at different points of the relationship. Serotonin levels become high when the initial excitement of the attraction phase wears off and your relationship begins to stabilize. At this time the increased serotonin produces a more comfortable feeling of love, known as attachment. These chemicals, rather than the soul mate myth, are what creates feelings of being "madly in love," romantically attached, or in a comfortable long-term relationship.

Nature Versus Nurture

Before we move on, it's a good time to remember that the idea of the soul mate is absolutely, positively based in fantasy. This idea seems untouchable and determined by forces out of our control, but it's best to let science triumph in this case. Now you know that when you meet someone and feel like it was destiny, that it's actually just a complicated string of biological processes that go to work when your body encounters another body. Granted, not just *any* body. But there will be quite a few times you experience that feeling in your lifetime. Certainly more than *one*. I could apologize for belittling what you experience as love—for making you feel *common* and your emotions less than extraordinary—but if you think about it, isn't that actually a comforting idea? Finding love is less of the mysterious, untouchable process than you thought. After all, if you're having a problem finding a man, wouldn't you rather try to balance your hormones, as discussed below, than try to take on the universe?

Love Enhancements

Are you "out of love"? Or are your hormones simply out of whack? Yes, it's a little scary to think that your experience of love is determined so much by all the processes taking place under your skin because the body is a sensitive and constantly changing thing. If love isn't this supernatural force, but rather a very scientific and material process, what happens when there is a glitch? Well, in many cases, people just think they have fallen out of love. While your naturally occurring hormones and neurotransmitters usually work just fine, it's possible to use either over-the-counter herbs or prescription drugs to either enhance your love life or help you overcome physical or mental barriers that are standing in your way of enjoying it. Before we go any further though, a word of caution: all chemical products, prescription and herbal, may have adverse reactions for some people. Do not use any of these products without first consulting your health care professional.

Long-Term Love

Often when one feels a lack of sexual desire they think it means that they have fallen out of love with their partner. But that's not necessarily the case. If you feel the passion in your relationship waning, this isn't because he isn't (gasp) "The One" and you've wasted all of this time with him. Rather their brain and body may simply be failing to produce the chemicals required for sexual desire and pleasure. When this happens, many people try to spice up their sex lives by seeking outside gratification. Why? Because the dopamine and phenylethylamine (PEA) rush that this new attraction produces can be mistaken for a new love. What you need to realize is that those chemicals will subside within six to eighteen months of the new attraction and then you've thrown away a valuable relationship for nothing. Since a long-term relationship is more than raging hormones and obsessive love, what is needed is a replacement for the chemicals that this new experience produces. The good news is that you can combine the stability of a long-term, established relationship with the *sensations* of a new one by trying the following supplements.

PRESCRIPTION ENHANCEMENTS

1. **Bupropion:** In the past, this drug has been used to treat depression and help people stop smoking, but it was recently approved to help with sexual dysfunction. Since the drug inhibits the re-uptake (by leaving them in the body longer, as they are not reabsorbed) of the sexual stimulant chemicals dopamine and norepinepherine, it is believed to offset the serotonin excess created by many anti-depressant drugs—a problem because seratonin excess tends to create such a feeling of calm and comfort, that it inhibits not only aggressive, but also sexual drives.

2. **Bremelanotide:** This substance primarily works by activating the areas of the brain involved in sexual behavior and dopamine production, which, in turn, increases female sexual desire.

3. **Estrogen:** This hormone often helps women who are post-menopausal in overcoming vaginal dryness. In pre-menopausal women it can also enhance sex drive.

4. **Testosterone:** When taken as a prescription, this hormone enhances sex drives in both women and men. But, the side effects include facial hair, muscular development, and an increased risk of heart disease and breast cancer.

5. **Viagra (Sildenafil Citrate):** In some studies Viagra enhanced genital blood flow, as well as vaginal and clitoral engorgement in women.

HERBAL ENHANCERS

1. **Macafem:** This dehydrated vegetable plant has been used as a substitute for hormone replacement therapy because it stimulates the pituitary gland into producing precursor hormones to raise estrogen, progesterone, and testosterone levels. Since these hormones are associated with high

sex drives, it makes sense to want to keep them in plentiful amounts in the body to get the most out of a sexual relationship.

2. **Ginseng:** This herb has been used for centuries to improve circulation. As a sexual enhancer, it helps in the secretion of nitric oxide, which causes the muscles to relax so that blood vessels can open up and allow more blood to flow into the genitals. Since this herb enhances sexuality by increasing circulation to the genitals it can be used by both men and women.

3. **Gingko Biloba:** Long known as the "memory herb," ginkgo biloba aids in both mental sharpness and sexual arousal by improving circulation and increasing blood flow to both the brain and the genitals. It also produces greater stimulation and sensitivity in the genitals for both men and women.

4. **L-Arginine:** This amino acid is needed to make nitric acid, which in turn relaxes blood vessels, allowing more blood to flow to the sexual organs.

5. **Dehydroepiandosterone (DHEA):** This hormone is naturally produced by the adrenal glands and is converted in the body to estrogen and testosterone. Since DHEA levels decrease with age, thereby causing sex hormones to decrease, DHEA supplements may boost the sex drive of post-menopausal women.

6. **Black Cohosh Root:** As estrogen levels decline in a woman's body during middle age, she may experience unpleasant symptoms such as mood swings, hot flashes, headaches, and vaginal dryness. These symptoms can cause a decrease in sexual arousal and responsiveness. Black cohosh root contains plant compounds called *phytoestrogens*, which bind to the estrogen receptors in the body, and help middle-aged women with their sexual desire and ability.

This plant offsets the above negative symptoms associated with menopause, thereby increasing a woman's overall good mood, as well as vaginal secretions that facilitate a woman's sex drive.

7. **Valerian Root:** This herb appears to be mainly effective due to its calming, anti-anxiety effects, which are important factors in the female sexual response. With less anxiety, a woman is better able to feel comfortable, enjoy sex, and bond with her partner, setting the stage for oxytocin release and the resulting feeling of attachment.

If you're looking into taking any of these drugs or supplements, please remember to clear this with your physician. But don't forget that sexual enhancers can magnify the experience of intimacy, thereby increasing production of the chemicals needed to solidify a romantic relationship. It's not a soul mate that keeps love—or sexual energy—alive. You're just feeling the effects of chemicals, which can be adjusted if needed. So now that you're familiar with some of the chemicals and hormones involved in feelings of love and attraction, you're ready to learn at what phases of your relationship each hormone plays a role. So keep reading!

Your Brain and Love

Hopefully by now you've learned that the connection you feel when you meet someone new isn't some inexplicable force, but actually biological and chemical reactions within your body. The progression of that initial attraction—or your love cycle—which ranges from feelings of attachment and even being in love is also the result of observable and particular factors like compatibility and trust. This combination of biology, compatibility, and the accumulation of pleasant moments with a person makes up the normal progression of the love cycle, which consists of several steps or phases:

- the attraction phase
- the romantic or honeymoon phase
- the attachment phase

You've felt them! Throughout these stages different parts of the brain dominate, and chemical reactions vary.

The Attraction Phase

In the late 1990s, Earl Naumann, author of the book *Love at First Sight* found that 65 percent of people believe in the phenomenon, and 50 percent claim to have experienced it. Don't think you have? Consider the following scenario: You walk into a crowded room and see someone hot on the other end. Your pupils dilate, your heart beats faster, and maybe you even begin to sweat a little as a rush of excitement and anticipation overwhelms you. Is it love at first sight? Well, perhaps. At the very least, it's lust.

Here's what's going on behind the scenes: When you see anyone you're attracted to, your body reacts in a predictable manner: after the visual cue enters through our optic nerve in the back of your eye, it goes to the *thalamus*, which is the brain's relay center. The thalamus sends it to the *neo-cortex* (or "thinking center") and to the *amygdala*, the seat of emotion and memories. The amygdala relays it to the *hypothalamus*. This part of the brain is closely linked to the *pituitary gland*, which controls endocrine functions. The pituitary gland then releases *neurotransmitters* and *endorphins*. The body then begins to react as if it's in fight or flight mode except in this case, it's flight towards an object (your hot guy), not away from one. Sounds good, right? Right! But before we go any further, let's first take a look at what role the senses play in attraction.

The Look of Love

For many of us, visual cues are often the most important factor when it comes to initial attraction. And, it should be no surprise that men and women are looking to satisfy different desires. Now, I'm sure you have a "type" that you prefer, but for the most part, women prefer larger, muscular men (guys like David Beckham, Matthew McConaughey, or Tom Selleck). Why is that? Well, back when we were cavewomen, these men were an asset because they offered more protection. Even if you tend to fall for the skinny jean-wearing types, it's interesting to know that researchers at UCLA recently found that while women chose "slim" versus "brawny" guys as the most sexually attractive, men who are more muscular than the average Joe were 166 percent more likely to have flings and multiple sex partners.

On the other hand, men are most attracted to hourglass figures and long, blonde hair. Think Emmy nominated actress Sofia Vergara and Marilyn Monroe. In 1993, Professor Devendra Singh at the University of Texas discovered that, despite the shrinking physical size of Playmates and Miss America contestants between 1957 and 1987, most of them had a waist-to-hip ratio between 0.68 and 0.71, meaning the ideal waist measurement is two thirds of the hip measurement. A desirable measurement is between 34-inch and 36-inch bust, 24-inch waist, and 34-inch hips. You can calculate your ratio here *www.healthstatus.com/calculate/whr*. (Women tend to be attracted to men with a waist-to-hip ratio around 0.9.) And, like it or not, the desire for a woman with child-bearing hips and larger breasts that speak to an ability to breastfeed more easily may not only make evolutionary sense but be backed up by actual science. Recently, a Polish study discovered that women with natural "Barbie doll" figures had 30 percent higher levels of the hormone estradiol, which is the precursor of estrogen, in their blood than did women who had other body shapes. Those levels of estradiol meant those women were three times easier to impregnate. So, for all you hourglass-shaped ladies, that's just another good reason to use protection.

But what's up with men being attracted to blondes? Evolution, again. As women get older, our hair darkens, so the male brain interprets blondes as younger and therefore, more fertile. In the book *Do Gentlemen Really Prefer Blondes?* Jena Pincott argues that this desire is rooted in evolutionary biases and that, in study after study, men will tend to claim greater attraction to the women with blonde hair, as opposed to the darker-haired women.

Now, I'm not suggesting you bleach your hair or do anything else to look like Barbie. Most women don't look like that and more attractive than a blonde head of hair and curvy figure is a woman who is completely comfortable with her natural assets.

So, lighter-haired ladies, don't be ashamed of your bright tresses. Use your appearance to draw men in but then impress them with your intellect and show them how your interests are compatible with theirs. Darker-haired damsels, grab your blonde or redheaded girlfriends and go out on the town. Your wing women will help attract the guys and you can easily turn on their brains and prove you're the keeper.

Many women build their ex-boyfriends up as the perfect man or the one who got away. If this sounds like you, consider why you two broke up in the first place. Are there issues that you and he are able to solve together or are you two just not compatible? Consider the reasons why you want to get back together. Is it loneliness, or do you miss having a boyfriend, someone familiar to talk with? If this is the case, you need to get involved in other activities. If many of your activities revolved around him, try some new things in which he wasn't involved. If you want to be back with him because you honestly miss him and think you two could work things out better the second time, then feel free to give it a go—just don't forget that he's not perfect.

The Scent of a Woman

Smell is the ultimate sex sense. To put it simply, you're attracted to someone who smells really good and repulsed by someone who smells bad. But if you think about it, in between those two extremes are people whose scent you would happily nuzzle for hours—in fact, in the past maybe you've even breathed in the scent of a pillow your lover was lying on as if their scent was your own personal Febreeze—and others you wouldn't. And interestingly, not everyone would feel the same way about that person's aroma. Or yours!

When it comes to scent, there's more going on than just what we can consciously recognize. Your brain detects odorless chemicals called pheromones that are released when you're attracted to someone new. Animals rely on pheromones too. They use them to mark territory, to signal aggression, to distinguish their offspring, and of course, when a female is alerting the males she's ready to mate. The use of pheromones isn't quite as obvious among humans, but they help explain why you have romantic chemistry with some people and not others. And your body will release pheromones in the presence of *many* men—not just a soul mate—because this is a chemical process that everyone is susceptible to. At puberty, the skin's sweat-producing glands starts to release these chemicals, which then accumulate in the eyelid, the nose, the lips, the pubic hair, and the underarm; basically the parts of the body that contain the most of these type of glands.

But, what determines who smells incredible to you or who you find yourself inexplicably drawn towards? Your genes. Often, we're attracted to people who possess a particular set of genes, known as the major histocompatibility complex (MHC), which plays a critical role in the ability to fight viruses. Mates with dissimilar MHC genes produce healthier offspring with broad immune systems. Think about it: if you carry genes that fight the cold well, and your partner carries genes that fight the flu well, your child will be armed with double the virus-fighting power. But if both you and your partner just possess the cold-fighting genes, you're not offering as much to your child. And science has revealed that we are inclined to choose people who suit us in this way—those with dissimilar MHC.

Within controlled studies, people tend to rate the scent of T-shirts worn by those with dissimilar MHC to their own as the most attractive. Apparently, there is some connection between your particular MHC and how your pheromones smell to another human. And, it's been found that couples tend to be less similar in their MHC than if random pairs of individuals were placed together and had their MHCs compared. Now just because you like what you smell next time you meet a guy doesn't mean you're meant to be together. There's a lot that has to go right for a romance to blossom: First the guy has to look attractive to you, just as he is standing across the room. But when you approach him, through the use of pheromones, your nose will tell you whether you'd actually want to go to bed with this person, or at the very least on a date. And finally, even if those first two steps are satisfied, the guy has to actually be single and likeable. But sorry, no chemical is going to tell you that. You just have to ask the guy and hope he tells the truth!

The truth is that compatible MHC can't overcome other practical obstacles. Even if you are chemically compatible, the romance may not be right. For example, if another person is leaving for active military duty, going away to college, speaks a different language, or is already in a committed relationship, the connection may end with attraction. Practical matters such as these can determine if one pursues the attraction into the romantic phase.

SINGLE LADIES

In 2005 ABC News took two sets of identical twins (one set of male twins and one set of female twins) who shared the same MHC speed dating to casually test the validity of pheromone sprays. One twin of each pair was given a perfume with pheromones added. The other was given a perfume without added pheromones. And, as it turned out, the effects of the perfume were so strong, that both the male and female twin wearing it received more attention from men. Other studies have backed up this experiment and discovered that women between the ages of twenty and fifty who wear the perfume receive more male attention and requests for dates than women of that age not wearing pheromone perfume. So, while pheromone spray isn't going to help you get a man who is interested in a relationship per say, it may help you attract more of them! You can continue the weeding-out process from there.

If you're single and dating you've likely played the game where you try to figure out if a guy you just met likes you. It can be difficult to see male indicators of interest, but here are some signs that a guy might be interested in getting to know you better:

- He maintains eye contact for more than two or three seconds.
- He smiles at you, even when he doesn't think you're looking at him.
- He speaks to you about personal issues, such as his family and activities that he enjoys, and he asks you about your personal life.
- He sometimes loses his train of thought when speaking to you. That is because he is so focused on impressing you and saying the right things, that he might not be as comfortable as if he was talking to a male friend or a girl in whom he was not interested.
- He changes his schedule so he's around at times when he knows you're available, e.g., he goes to the gym at the time you go.
- Most important, he asks you to do something with him. Regardless of whether it is an activity with just the two of you, or something involving a group of people, the main point is that he shows an interest in spending more time with you.

The Romantic or Honeymoon Phase

As you progress from the initial meeting to a long-term, monogamous relationship with someone, the hormones and neurotransmitters that your brain releases change. At the romantic stage norepinephrine, dopamine, and PEA are still high but serotonin levels drop to levels similar to the levels of those who experience obsessive-compulsive disorder, and not surprisingly, you become obsessed with your love interest. During the orgasm in this phase, the parts of the brain known as the caudate nucleus—a part that is highly stimulated by the chemical dopamine—lights up, and oxytocin and PEA flood the body immediately afterwards producing feelings of intense pleasure. That is the reason for the intense feelings of pleasure during orgasm.

During this exciting, butterflies-in-the-stomach phase when lust and passion are high, the primary chemicals buzzing through your blood are dopamine, testosterone, norepinephrine, and phenylethylamine. Ever felt like you're almost physically addicted to your partner? The hormones released during this phase are some of the same released by some addictive drugs, like cocaine.

For most of us, this phase can't last forever. It's too exhausting! But while, for the majority of people, the chemical composition of love changes sometime between fifteen months and three years, for others the honeymoon just keeps on going. . . .

One Long Honeymoon

For some lucky couples, the positive feelings of the romantic phase last throughout their entire relationship. At the State University of New York at Stony Brook, a handful of young people who had just fallen madly in love volunteered to have their brain scanned to see what areas were active when they looked at pictures of their sweethearts. The areas that lit up were those known to be rich in dopamine, the pleasure chemical.

Those results aren't surprising, but when older volunteers who said they were still intensely in love after two decades of marriage had their brains scanned, the same brain areas lit up just as intensely. But, in these couples, areas rich in oxytocin, the cuddle or affection chemical, lit up as well, which strongly suggests that long-term passion is not only the result of an attraction towards each other but a deeper, more profound connection.

Though we're far off from being able to translate all of our romantic feelings into chemicals, scientists do know that dopamine plays a big role in the excitement of love and oxytocin is key for the calmer experience of attachment. And in the future, it's possible that, as neurobiologist Larry J. Young pointed out recently in *Nature*, once scientists understand the chemistry of love, drugs to manipulate the process "may not be far away." If the sensations we associate with finding a soul mate can in fact be chemically produced, then that is strong evidence against the idea that there is only one person with whom you can feel that connection.

WHAT CAN LOVE DO FOR YOUR BODY?

Love, whether you're in an extended honeymoon stage or not, can do amazing things for your body. Here's just a small sampling of what the power of love can do for you:

- Lower heart rate
- Improve your immune system
- Relieve stress, pain, and depression
- Promote deeper sleep
- Increase weight loss
- Stabilize hormone production

All of these factors signify and are key to maintaining good physical health.

The Attachment Phase

During this phase love becomes less obsessive and more comfortable. Those who mistakenly believe in the soul mate myth may think they have fallen out of love with their partner at this point. That is why it is important to understand that the varying levels of chemicals is a normal process in the progression towards a deepening relationship. It is a sign of committed love, not a symptom of disillusionment.

During this final stage, serotonin levels rise, leading to a decrease in the crazed feeling, and dopamine, norepinephrine, and PEA levels drop, leading to a calmer, more stable feeling of love. Simultaneously, vasopressin (the male attachment hormone that is found in higher quantities in men who are in committed relationships than in those who are not) and oxytocin (the cuddle chemical) levels increase. The result is that the couple, if they choose, are able to build a strong attachment to each other and perhaps experience long-term love.

When the Chemistry Is Wrong

Sometimes, even though you're attracted to someone, the chemistry is just . . . off. You may not want to be close or have any physical contact with them. That may be your body telling you this person isn't a good long-term partner because of what you can't see—their genes!

Often when a date does not work out, it does not mean that the person is not your "soul mate." Instead, remember that your immune system may be too similar and your pheromones therefore do not appeal to one another. For instance, have you ever seen a guy on a dating site and thought, "Wow! He's so hot! I want to go out with him!" Then, when you do, the date is flat?

A male patient once told me, "I met a woman in a bar when I was a bit drunk. She was quite attractive, so I suggested we go out one night. We went for dinner and had a great time. When we left, we walked along and began snuggling up together. We started hugging and kissing. Something felt wrong, that feeling just wasn't there. Still, I invited her out the next week. She turned me down saying there was no spark. I guess it wasn't just me." Despite the initial attraction, it was clear that when this man was sober his chemicals were letting him know that this woman wasn't a good match.

In the end, beer goggles and a pretty face can't override your body's natural warning signals. Your feelings of attraction dictated by your body chemistry often have the final word in whether or not you go on a second date.

SOUL MATE SCENARIOS:
Carol and Kyle

Carol and Kyle had been friends for a few months when Kyle wanted to see what it would be like to become more than friends. He asked Carol out on a double date and he kissed her. Oddly enough, although Kyle had all the characteristics Carol desired in a man—intelligence, wealth, good looks, chivalry, and a great sense of humor—she didn't feel sexually attracted to him. She told herself maybe it was just because she was used to seeing him as a friend. The next day, Carol woke up with a headache, muscle aches, and a sore throat. When she received a phone call from Kyle, his first words were, "This feels like the bubonic plague." The weird thing is, their other friends who came on the date and must have also been exposed to the virus did not get sick. So, what happened? Carol and Kyle's immune systems were likely very similar, which not only made them equally susceptible to the same virus, but it is also why Carol did not feel sexually attracted to Kyle. Remember that set of genes called MHC that determines your body's ability to fight off viruses? Carol and Kyle's MHC were too similar, meaning the pheromones they generated were similar as well. Your body naturally rejects sexual partners with similar MHC because if you were to reproduce with this person, your child would have a weaker immune system.

LESSON: There's a biological reason sometimes you just want to be friends with a guy. We tend to be romantically attracted to people that are our MHC opposites. That's good because it helps us partner with people who help us create a diverse gene pool.

THE PILL

On the surface, the birth control pill is a great means for preventing contraception within a monogamous relationship. But—and this is a big one—some scientists have found that women on the pill seem to prefer men with MHC similar to their own. Imagine the issues this might cause when a woman stops taking the pill and wants to have children? Suddenly, her partner isn't who she wants at all! The pill can also cause romantic rifts between a couple if a woman gets on the pill after a couple starts dating. She may then feel less attraction to the man with the opposite MHC, even though he might be a good match!

Soul Mate Summary

This chapter has given you a lot of insight into the real chemistry behind "love chemistry" and the important roles your brain plays in forming relationships and creating lasting love. Next we'll begin to face the fears that might be preventing you from having a lasting relationship. But first, in a nutshell, here's what we covered in this chapter:

- Invisible odors called pheromones help you attract a suitable partner. These chemicals are secreted by glands in your body that are in close proximity to erotic areas.

- There are different chemical processes that affect your brain throughout love's three stages: the attraction phase, the romantic phase, and the attachment phase. In the attraction phase, one feels an initial sexual excitement and desire to approach another person. Chemicals norepinephrine, phenylethylamine (PEA), and dopamine are high. During the romantic phase, dopamine, PEA, testosterone, and estrogen are high. Seratonin is low, leading to feelings of obsessive love. Later, in about six to eighteen months, the attachment phase begins. Seratonin is high, oxytocin is high in both men and women, and vasopressin is high in men. This leads to a deeper, although calmer, sense of love.

- The different hormones your body releases when you're aroused or falling for someone include estrogen for women, testosterone for both men and women, norepinephrine for both men and women, as well as other hormones that are associated with the later stage of romance known as attachment.

- Sexual enhancers are available for both men and women to increase desire and pleasure. These products may offset the lack of natural sex hormones in a person.

- These biological and chemical factors explain much of the mystery behind romantic love. The preceding chapter has provided much evidence for scientific factors, as opposed to the soul mate myth, as the ultimate determinants of attraction, romance, and long-term love.

CHAPTER 3

The Fear Barrier

Fear is what prevents you from beginning and maintaining a relationship with a good guy. When women are searching for the impossible-to-find soul mate, they often push away perfectly good men because they are still searching for that "perfect man." They fear that if they stay with this good guy, he will just stand in the way of their soul mate search.

When you feel yourself starting to like a man, do you begin to focus on his negative traits? Do you start fights when there really isn't any drama between you and your partner? Unless you want to be known as a drama queen, it's time to face the fact that something's been holding you back from being in a happy, loving relationship and that something might be *you*. Well, okay, maybe not *you*, but your *fears* may be pushing good partners away. Often when someone—in this case, you—has a desire to get close to others but is letting their fears dominate their thinking, they interact with others in such a way that gets them treated in the way they most feared. You think someone might leave, so you cling to them. You fear rejection so you're cold to your partner. You avoid dating because you believe that "all the good ones are taken," and so on. In psychology, this is called a self-fulfilling prophecy, but here you'll learn why you have these irrational fears, how to take control of the different types of fears that are holding you back, and how to change these destructive behaviors.

Why the Irrational Thinking?

Every time you have an experience, you judge and label it—good or bad, painful or pleasurable, safe or dangerous—based on what you've learned from your family, peers, and previous life experiences. We all continually make judgments and emotional decisions, and this "self-talk" is much of what makes up your internal dialogue. Self-talk is that voice in your head that speaks to you in the second person. It says things such as "you'll never succeed," "you'll never find the right guy," or "you're just not attractive enough." Self-talk can also be the voice that makes irrational statements, such as, "he should behave differently towards me" or "all men are no good." It's often composed of just a few words or a fleeting visual image that collects memories and feelings under one umbrella.

But, when these "automatic" thoughts are irrational, those images or words sometimes group together painful memories, fears, or self-reproaches. It's good to learn from your experiences so you can recognize a potentially negative event and protect yourself, but you should pay close attention to what it means to protect yourself and what it means to simply be paranoid or even cynical. Just because a certain situation played out one way once, doesn't mean that that type of situation will always play out that way. You may have had an ex who cheated on you and started using late "business meetings" as an excuse for staying out all night. In your next relationship, if your partner starts going to late business meetings, you may become paranoid that he is cheating on you too. But it's important, when those fears that developed from past experiences are creeping up, to stop and ask yourself, "who is *this* man? Would he really do that?" You need to take the guy's entire character into consideration before jumping to possibly damaging conclusions. Otherwise, you could just cause yourself a lot of needless anxiety. Ever played the "what if" game? Just take the words "What if" and start inserting a terrible idea or fear after it. "What if I never get married?" "What if my partner cheats on me?" "What if the sky falls?" These are examples of irrational thoughts. Some other examples include:

- It would be terrible to be rejected, abandoned, or alone. I must have love and approval before I can feel good about myself.
- If my partner criticizes me, it means there's something wrong with me.
- I must always please my partner and live up to his expectations.
- I am basically defective and inferior to other women.
- Men who don't treat me the way I wish to be treated are to blame for my problems.
- Men should always meet my expectations.
- It's not safe to feel happy and optimistic about a man because I will get burned.
- I'm hopeless and bound to feel depressed forever because I'll never find Mr. Right.

If this sounds like you, it seems that you sometimes let these pessimistic irrational fears—many of which are as realistic as the sky falling on your head—to take control of your brain, and with it, your emotions. Then, rather than learning to navigate your fears and insecurities, you tell yourself that there is a man out there with whom those insecurities will simply never rise to the surface. But this isn't true because it isn't anything on the outside that is provoking these fears. They are coming from inside of you and until you learn to deal with them, they will come out no matter who you are in a relationship with.

SINGLE LADIES

According to TopDatingTips.com, of the 2,000 people they polled, 42 percent of women and 34 percent of men thought the man should always pay for the date. However, after a few dates, it's not uncommon for the woman to reciprocate either by taking him out to dinner, to a game, or somewhere he would enjoy, or cooking him a fantastic meal.

Common Cognitive Distortions

Your senses don't want to distort reality and create irrational thoughts and fears. However, between the transmission from your auditory and occipital nerves to your brain, then to your hypothalamus (the part of your brain that processes information from the senses), and finally to your nervous system, which produces the chemicals that affect your behavior, there is much possibility for distortion. This process is complex and is influenced by your brain and body chemistry, your prior experiences, your brain's interpretation of the sensory input, and your interactions with the other people in your life and environment. The following sections tell you when it's important to take another look at what's provoking your fears.

Should Statements

When you use "should statements" you tell yourself that things should be the way you hoped or expected them to be. "Musts," "oughts," and "have tos," like the following are similar offenders:

- My partner should understand my needs without my having to tell him.
- My partner should share all my interests and activities, as a good soul mate would.
- I need to find my soul mate to be satisfied sexually, so we can have simultaneous orgasms.

Such statements directed against the self lead to guilt and frustration while should statements against others or external circumstances lead to anger and frustration. It's a cute idea that you and your partner will always be on the same page. That you'll find the same things annoying, thrilling, boring, etc. And obviously, *sometimes* that will happen, and it makes you feel bonded when it does. But a premise behind the soul mate myth is that you two will *always* share the same feelings and opinions. So if you buy into the myth, you think it's a bad match the second the two of you disagree. Since two people are never exactly alike, the premise behind the soul mate myth leads to the very unhappiness that it is designed to prevent.

Labeling

Labeling is an extreme form of overgeneralizing where you equate yourself with your actions. For example, instead of saying, "I made a mistake. It happens," you attach a negative label to your self such as, "I'm a loser." Granted your actions can define you, but one action does not make the woman. Think about the most successful person you know—they can be famous or just someone in your life—and imagine they make a mistake. Maybe they miss a meeting or they get a parking ticket or they get dumped. Do you now think this person is a loser and no longer successful? Chances are you don't feel that way. You likely wouldn't judge another person in such a harsh light, and you shouldn't judge yourself so harshly either.

That said, if you *would* judge someone else that harshly if they did something that rubs you the wrong way, you may need to start to change your thought patterns. This type of thinking can easily lead to hostile feelings, hopelessness or disappointment about them, and as a result, leave little room for constructive communication. If you push everyone away that makes one mistake, you will end up a very lonely person. Now, you shouldn't be spineless and forgive every mistake a person makes, but you should try to find a balance and take the time to figure out how representative that mistake really was of the person as a whole.

Personalization/Blame

Personalization or blame is when you hold yourself—or someone else—personally responsible for an event that isn't entirely under your control. For example, when one woman's husband constantly criticized her, she told herself, "If only I were better in bed, he wouldn't pick on me." Personalization leads to guilt, shame, and feelings of inadequacy. Some people do the opposite. They blame *other* people or their circumstances for their problems, and then overlook ways that *they* might be contributing to the problem: "The reason my marriage is so lousy is because my spouse is totally unreasonable." What all these ideas come down to is the basic premise that, "If I could only find my soul mate, he would understand exactly what I need and give it to me. We would then have eternal happiness together." But, as you've seen before, no two people are exactly alike. Harmony in a relationship requires constant work and understanding. No two separate people will ever come together and effortlessly live in harmony every second. It's just not possible. You and your partner may have a lot in common, but you're not the same person, and sometimes your desires are going to conflict. But conflict is never caused by just one person; both partners contribute to the issue, which means you could be a part of the problem.

Black-and-White Thinking

Have you felt that, if something falls short of perfect, it's a total failure? For instance, let's imagine you have a hot date tonight. You hope that your lover will show up on time, with flowers, kiss you when he arrives, and take you out for a fun night on the town. They do all of the above and you have a great time, except they didn't bring you flowers. Was the night a failure? Of course not! But if you focus on the one thing that wasn't done, you run the risk of ruining a good thing for yourself. This type of black-and-white thinking not only causes you frustration and unnecessary disappointment, but it also puts a ridiculous amount of pressure on you and/or your partner to perform your unspoken desires exactly as you envisioned them. If you overidealize your man, you set him up for failure. At the first sign of imperfection, you fall out of love with him. To prevent black-and-white thinking, you need to understand that no person, including your partner, is either totally wonderful or a complete louse. Rather, all human beings are a combination of both wonderful and lousy traits, and display these traits at varying times in varying degrees.

Overgeneralization

When you overgeneralize, you take a single negative event, such as a romantic rejection, and believe it has launched a never-ending pattern of defeat by using words such as "always" or "never" when you think about those type of situations. For example, you were just dumped. Guess you'll never ever have another boyfriend, right? Yeah . . . that sounds logical.

Mental Filter

If you have a mental filter you pick out a single negative detail and dwell on it exclusively, so that your vision of all of reality becomes darkened. You focus on the one problematic aspect of your relationship. For instance, your partner often forgets to clean up the sink after he's shaved. Instead of seeing all of his great qualities, this is the one you focus on. Not surprisingly, it causes conflict and strife. This mental filter when turned towards the self can also cause dissatisfaction and low self-esteem. This is something difficult for your partner to deal with, too. If you make one little mistake and are relentlessly hard on yourself for it, it's easy for your partner to feel helpless in making you feel better about yourself because you seem incapable of seeing your own good qualities. And if you constantly see things through this mental filter, your partner might start to feel like they're never going to live up to your expectations and they might become resentful. They'll feel they'll never be good enough for you or that they will never be able to make you feel good about yourself. Now the man of your dreams, your hypothetical soul mate, would make you feel so good about yourself that you would never notice your own flaws, and he wouldn't have any of his own. But this man only appears perfect because he is hypothetical. If every man you meet seems to be imperfect, that is because he is. This is the reason why you cannot find this nonexistent soul mate creature.

Discounting the Positive

If you commonly discount the positive, you probably struggle to enjoy otherwise pleasant experiences because you tell yourself they "don't count." While you fixate on the negative qualities of your partner, it makes you incapable of enjoying any nice experiences you have together. For example, if your partner constantly forgets to clean the kitchen, and one night he makes you an amazing surprise dinner, but forgets to clean the kitchen as usual, you don't appreciate the dinner, but only focus on that dirty kitchen. When he is clearly displaying generosity and thoughtfulness, all you see is carelessness. This, just like the mental filter, will make your partner feel unappreciated and constantly inadequate.

Jumping to Conclusions

Chances are you have, at one point or another, jumped to conclusions about something that's gone on in your life. Let's be honest here; almost everyone has. But if you make a habit out of it, this cognitive distortion becomes problematic. After all, what good could come out of interpreting things negatively when there aren't any facts to support your conclusion?

There are two specific types of this cognitive distortion: mind reading and fortune telling. When you mind read you decide that you know what someone else is thinking and assume that they are reacting negatively to you. When you fortune tell, you predict that things will turn out badly. Both mind reading and fortune telling have the same repercussions: they do not work. Since they both depend upon magic and fantasy, they are doomed to fail just like the soul mate myth. And like the soul mate myth both mind reading and fortune telling can sabotage good relationships. If you "fortune tell" that your boyfriend is going to be late to dinner and you treat him badly based on this fortune, that can only lead to conflict because you are punishing him for a crime he has yet to commit, and maybe even won't. If you "mind read" that your boyfriend finds you unattractive one night, you might act distant because you feel insecure, and he will read your distance as you wanting space and then he will give you even less of the attention that you actually really need at that moment. Fortune telling, mind reading, and the soul mate myth are all in your head. However, believing in them can have damaging effects on the real people and events in your life.

RATIONAL THINKING QUIZ

Now that you know all about these common cognitive distortions and how they could be standing in the way of having a good guy in life, let's explore where you stand on the scale of rational thinking.

1. My friends should do what I want them to do.   True   False

2. Criminals are bad people.   True   False

3. If I was a better wife, my husband wouldn't have divorced me.
   True   False

4. I want everything just the way I want it.   True   False

5. I always get the raw end of the deal.   True   False

6. My partner is a slob because he throws his clothes on the floor.
   True   False

7. So what if I like my job! It doesn't matter if I don't earn enough money.
   True   False

8. Because he was late for our date, he must not like me.   True   False

9. People should never lie.   True   False

10. My partner must believe in my religion.   True   False

11. It's my parents' fault I don't have better relationships.   True   False

12. If I don't get married by the time I'm thirty, I'll never get married.
    True   False

13. Because we don't have sex enough, our relationship is no good.
    True   False

14. That good time we had was a farce.   True   False

15. He looked away. He must not be interested.   True   False

16. I should have known better.   True   False

17. All men who spend a lot of time on their appearance are no good.
    True   False

18. It's my fault that I'm not smart enough.   True   False

19. You're either good or no good.   True   False

20. If my date comes late, he is disrespecting me.   True   False

21. The way he dresses proves he's not the right one.   True   False

22. My parents were no good.   True   False

23. If he doesn't know that, he must be stupid.   True   False

24. I should always get excellent ratings at work.   True   False

25. I am stupid.   True   False

26. I would have had a better life if I hadn't married him.   True   False

27. If he didn't buy me a birthday gift, he's a jerk.   True   False

28. My parents divorced so that means I'll get divorced.   True   False

29. I'm alone this weekend and it's terrible.   True   False

30. That club can't be any good if they have me as a member.   True   False

31. He didn't come home on time so he must hate me.   True   False

32. I should be married by now.   True   False

33. If I am not married, I'm a haggard old spinster.   True   False

34. I'm no good, that's why I'm not married.   True   False

35. All the good men are taken.   True   False

36. I'll never find a good man.   True   False

37. Our relationship is no good because we hardly kiss.   True   False

38. So what if he brought me flowers, flowers are cheap.   True   False

39. He didn't bring me flowers so he doesn't love me.   True   False

Scoring

Give your self one point for every true and zero points for every false.

Interpretation

If your total score is between 0 and 10, congratulations, you're probably very rational. If it's between 11 and 20, it's average, with some weak areas. If it's 21 to 30, you have some moderate difficulty with being rational. And if it's between 31 and 39, you have some difficulty with irrational thoughts and need to focus on overcoming your cognitive distortions before you commit to being in a happy, loving relationship with someone else. To be ready for a serious relationship, you must have a core of inner stability and rationality. Otherwise, your intense negative emotions will destroy the relationship at the first sign of disagreement or stress.

ALL IN MODERATION

You may have put a check mark next to some of the fears we just discussed and are now sitting there thinking, "Well. I'm a basket case." But rest assured, almost everyone experiences one if not all of the fears and self-imposed mind games discussed in this chapter to some degree. Being in love *does* make you vulnerable, so of course there will be some fears. The problems only arise when that fear is so strong, that it consistently interferes with or even destroys your relationships.

Break It Down

Use this quiz to get an idea of how you could change your thinking. Because you really need to be able to face the facts and get honest about what you need to address, let's break your answers down into the different cognitive disorder categories so you know what areas you really need to focus on. This will help you work to overcome your specific barriers to a relationship with a good man.

Look at questions 1, 9, 17, 25, and 33. If you answered true to three or more of these, you may tend to make should/must/etc. statements.

Look at questions 2, 10, 18, 26, and 34. If you answered true to three or more of these, you may tend to label or mislabel people or situations.

Look at questions 3, 11, 19, 27, and 35. If you answered true to three or more of these, you may tend to blame others or personalize problems.

Look at questions 4, 12, 20, 28, and 36. If you answered true to three or more of these, you may tend to think about situations or people in black-and-white.

Look at questions 5, 13, 21, 29, and 37. If you answered true to three or more of these, you may tend to overgeneralize.

Look at questions 5, 14, 22, 32, and 38. If you answered true to three or more of these, you may tend to put a mental filter on things.

Look at questions 7, 15, 23, 31, and 39. If you answered true to three or more of these, you may tend to discount the positive.

Look at questions 8, 16, 24, 32, and 39. If you answered true to three or more of these, you may tend to jump to conclusions.

Now that you have a good idea where your problems lie, let's take a look at some of the fears that you may have created by thinking irrationally. Thinking leads to action, so your irrational thoughts have most likely manifested themselves into actions on your part that have been damaging to relationships.

How long should you wait before you text or call a new guy? Within a day or two, feel free to give the guy a call and say something like, "I enjoyed (such and such event) yesterday. It would be great to see you again." Don't text him twice in a row if he doesn't text back; you want to make sure there's a balance of power and don't want to harass him with constant texting or communication.

The Primary Relationship Fears

As you can see, there are a lot of irrational relationship fears out there. But, underneath all of them is a general fear of intimacy, of getting too close to a partner physically and/or emotionally and having that relationship not work out. If you are a woman who is having trouble finding a date, you need to understand that being too picky, and seeking the perfect partner or soul mate, can be a way to avoid confronting your fears about possible disappointment or rejection. What's tricky is that you can be married or committed to a partner but not feel emotionally intimate. If you feel lonely even though you're in a partnership or feel a great distance between you and your partner, one of you might be suffering from a fear of intimacy. Since intimacy and authenticity are the two biggest building blocks for a healthy, fulfilling romantic relationship, it's important that you begin to work through your fears and move towards something will actually make you happy. Granted, relationship fears are more difficult to work on than those you're likely more used to tackling—things like a fear of spiders, fear of flying, or fear of the unknown—but, like any emotional wound, the healing needs to start from within you.

Below you'll find information on the six primary relationship fears that can contribute to a fear of intimacy and some techniques you can use to talk yourself out of irrational beliefs, unravel your issues, and start searching for a good relationship. These techniques are all based on the concept of cognitive behavioral therapy (CBT) also known as rational emotive therapy. CBT works off the idea that your irrational thoughts about a situation are, in fact, a distortion in thinking that leads to negative emotions like anger, fear, depression, and guilt when the situation at hand shouldn't actually elicit that type of emotional reaction. CBT helps you dispute the irrational thoughts behind intense negative emotions; and substitute rational thoughts, which in turn lead to less intense negative emotions and more positive feelings. Through CBT, you can learn to change these thought patterns and turn down the volume or intensity of these negative emotions. You'll be able to turn anger into reasonable irritation, turn fear into healthy hesitation, turn feelings of depression into momentary sadness, turn guilt into something you can learn from for the future, and turn demands of your partner into preferences.

So without further ado, let's tackle your fears!

Fear of Engulfment

Famed Freudian psychoanalyst Karen Horney wrote that we have three ways of dealing with others: moving towards them, moving away from them, and moving against them. Those who suffer from a fear of engulfment have never learned how to balance these skills. They feel so overwhelmed and overpowered in early family relationships that their only alternative seems to be complete surrender or destruction of their self or of others. Having a turbulent childhood or family ties could make them shun romantic ties later in life. From a behavioral standpoint, they have no practice at asserting their own needs in intimate relationships because they were not given much of a chance to do this as a child. Therefore, they tend to avoid getting close to anyone. If you believe that getting involved in a relationship with someone else might cause your identity to be swallowed up, it might mean you have a fear of engulfment that is holding you back from having deep, meaningful romantic relationships and perhaps has prevented you from engaging in one altogether.

Signs you suffer from a fear of engulfment:

- You worry that if you become too deeply invested in a relationship you might lose your identity.
- You believe that your relationship will interfere with your other responsibilities.
- You often have a need to "get away" from your partner.
- You feel most comfortable with people with whom you know you'll be granted whatever degree of personal space you desire.

Where Does This Come From?

Sometimes this fear is the result of having parents who were ill-equipped to help you build a sense of self and cope with the external world. For example, if your parent was an alcoholic who constantly needed your assistance, or if you had a single mother who was going through breakups that you had to nurse her through, you might fear intimacy because you don't want the responsibility of someone else's feelings getting in the way of your development and identity. Sometimes the opposite is the case and your parent was very strict and you felt that your desires and emotions were not taken into consideration. If this is the case, later in life you may feel more at ease when left alone without worry of being intruded upon or suffocated again.

One last somewhat obvious but very strong cause of fear of intimacy is if, as a child, you observed your parents fight often. Children subconsciously consider their parents' marriage as an example of what most marriages are like. If you were constantly exposed to a turbulent romantic relationship of your parents, your overwhelming impression of relationships may be that they are more turbulent than peaceful. This fear doesn't only develop out of childhood experiences, however. If you yourself have experienced a turbulent relationship, breakup up, or divorce, those experiences can also cause you to develop a fear of intimacy.

FEAR OF ENGULFMENT QUIZ

Take the following quiz to find out if you have a fear of engulfment. As you take the quiz, be honest with yourself. If a statement applies to your life very often, circle 1. If it applies sometimes, circle 2. If it applies rarely, circle 3. And, if it never applies or applies only very rarely under certain circumstances, circle 4.

	OFTEN	SOMETIMES	RARELY	NEVER
When I am in a close relationship I worry about the other person controlling me.	1	2	3	4
I feel that being in a relationship will interfere with the goals that I want to accomplish.	1	2	3	4
I am usually accepting of most things about people that I know intimately.	1	2	3	4
I am afraid that I will not live up to my partner's standards.	1	2	3	4
I can't remain faithful to one partner forever.	1	2	3	4
I know that intimacy brings up both good and bad feelings and I am willing to take the good with the bad.	1	2	3	4

Scoring

For questions 1, 2, 4, and 5 give yourself one point for every 1, two points for every 2, three points for every 3, and four points for every 4. For the remaining questions, give yourself four points for every 1, three points for every 2, two points for every 3, and one point for every 4.

Interpretation

Add the points for questions 1 through 6. If your score is 6 to 12 you have a significant fear of engulfment. If your score is 13 to 18, your fear of engulfment is average. If your score is 19 to 24, you have no real fear of engulfment.

SOUL MATE SCENARIOS:
Lynette

Lynette was in her late twenties and engaged to Doug, who was in his late thirties. Lynette was a teacher living in New York. Doug was a sports writer, living in Los Angeles. They enjoyed a long-term relationship, which consisted of spending weekends together once a month. They took turns, so one month Lynette would fly to Los Angeles and the next month Doug would fly to New York. They shared almost daily telephone and e-mail contacts, and every so often Lynette would complain to friends that she wished they could spend more time together.

Then, one day, Doug called with exciting news. He was being transferred to New York! Lynette told him she was so excited and couldn't wait until the two of them could spend more time together. She mentioned, that if it worked for him, that he could stay with her until he found a suitable place to live. But, then, that night—and for the next few days—Lynette felt plagued by anxiety. She was excited, but also felt that him moving to New York and staying in her apartment would mean that she'd lose her identity. Would she have to stop going out with her friends? Would her job suffer? Would she have to give up the life she loved? She started to panic; exhibiting a real fear of engulfment.

LESSON: There is always a certain amount of compromise in every relationship. You do need to dedicate time and attention to your partner if you really want to feel closeness. Finding that right balance between being a committed partner and still keeping your individual identity isn't always easy. But if you simply avoid the challenge of finding that balance all together by ending every relationship that gets serious, you are cheating yourself out of a long-term relationship.

ARE YOU IN A "VACATION-ONLY RELATIONSHIP"?

Long-distance relationships can work out. However, what you want to avoid is having what some call a "vacation-only relationship." This is a relationship in which you only experience one another when you are both completely free of responsibilities, and you are not able to get a real sense of what it would be like to be with this person on a day-to-day basis, with both of your stresses playing a role in the relationship. To test the strength of your long distance relationship, have your partner visit you for an extended period of time, when you will be going to work regularly, and vice versa.

Treating Your Fear of Engulfment

To begin to address your own fears of engulfment, start by asking yourself, what is the worst-case scenario that could occur if you were to allow yourself to become intimate with someone? In most cases, the worst that would happen is the relationship might not work out. But, there is also a much greater possibility that if you do not allow yourself to be intimate with a partner—either emotionally or physically—that they will not stick around. If you don't allow yourself to become intimate with a partner due to your fears, or desire for perfection, you often let the good guys slip away, as you wait for your fantasy mate.

That being said, fear of engulfment is one fear that doesn't completely fall into the category of irrational.

When you're in a relationship, it's important to keep in mind that both you and your partner should maintain some independence. People really *can* become engulfed. Love is exciting and it can be distracting; some people stop seeing their friends as often, become distracted from their career, or just generally neglect other parts of their life in favor of snuggling up with their partner. If you're afraid that you have a tendency to become engulfed, just be sure to be ultra aware of that and force yourself, even when it's tough, to disentangle yourself from your partner and go out for a drink with your friends, or work on that project for work—whatever it may be. You'll both be happier if you do.

Please keep in mind that the treatments you'll find both here and throughout this chapter aren't just one-time exercises. They're lifetime projects. Employ them whenever you feel you're starting to go back to your old ways. If any of these questions really hit home for you, write them down and keep them somewhere where you can see them. So the next time you're about to pick a fight with your partner or do anything that might drastically affect the relationship, go look at those questions and see if it is just one of your fears that is provoking your behavior. And, if you don't see progress from these treatments but still feel that you're wrestling with your fears, seriously consider seeking cognitive behavioral therapy. Improving your relationship with yourself is the most important thing you can do to improve your present and future relationships with others.

Signs you are progressing past your fear of engulfment:

- You're interested in dating and you're making choices that will put you on that path.
- You have decided to take dating seriously or you are seeing someone seriously.
- You're willing to spend your weekends with your partner.
- You feel comfortable discussing future plans with your partner.
- When your partner brings up issues, you now feel more comfortable talking them out and you get less emotionally overwhelmed in those circumstances.

Fear of Commitment

You may have heard of or even dated some guys who say they have a "fear of commitment." Well, even though a lot of men use this catch phrase as a way of continuing to not settle down or hold on to their youth, some people do have a real fear of commitment. These people are often unwilling to work out relationship issues in healthy ways because, if they do, they know they might want to remain within the relationship—and all those exciting nights out and one-night stands and a relationship don't really mix. For women, this often exhibits itself in the desire to not "settle" for someone who doesn't exactly meet their expectations—who isn't their soul mate. So don't set your expectations so high that you let all the good ones get away.

Signs you suffer from a fear of commitment:
- You resent having to give up some of your freedom and independence to be intimate with a romantic partner.
- You get involved in relationships that you know will be limited by time or other factors.
- You get involved with people you are comfortable with but with whom you don't believe you could have a long-term commitment with.
- When you do find a good or great match, you work to see all of their negative traits so they no longer seem like a good match for you.
- You're afraid of "settling," so when you're in relationships you're often on the lookout for someone better.

Where Does This Come From?

A fear of commitment comes from a fear of responsibility and an inability to tolerate stress. This person was often allowed a lot of freedom in their family of origin. They could come and go as they pleased; and they were free to just walk away from uncomfortable situations. Whether it was a strict teacher or a relative that they disliked, their parents often did not enforce the need to stick to a strict regimen. They would let the kid skip class, or wouldn't force them to visit that disliked relative. Therefore, the person with fear of commitment was often able to pick up and leave when the going got tough, so they never developed the skills for dealing with conflict and pressure.

FEAR OF COMMITMENT QUIZ

Take the following quiz to find out if you have a fear of commitment. As you take the quiz, be honest with yourself. If a statement applies to your life very often, circle 1. If it applies sometimes, circle 2. If it applies rarely, circle 3. And, if it never applies or applies only very rarely under certain circumstances, circle 4.

	OFTEN	SOMETIMES	RARELY	NEVER
I am willing to do everything I can to support my partner.	1	2	3	4
I can accept the fact that in a committed relationship I may occasionally have to sacrifice my own interests.	1	2	3	4
When I am in a relationship it takes priority over any other aspect in my life.	1	2	3	4
I derive a great amount of satisfaction from being involved with one person.	1	2	3	4
One of the dangers of becoming close to someone is that you become more vulnerable to manipulation.	1	2	3	4
I worry about growing old and being alone.	1	2	3	4

Scoring

For questions 1, 2, 3, 4, and 6 give yourself four points for every 1, three points for every 2, two points for every 3, and one point for every 4. For the remaining question, give yourself one point for a 1, two points for a 2, three points for a 3, and four points for a 4.

Interpretation

Add the points for questions 1 through 6. If your score is 6 to 12, you have a significant fear of commitment. If your score is 13 to 18, your fear of commitment is within the average range. If your score is 19 to 24, you have no real fear of commitment.

SOUL MATE SCENARIOS:
Betty

Betty, an attractive woman in her early twenties, had dated many men but had disposed of all of them over minor infractions. In one case, she dumped a boyfriend because his work-related duties prevented him from accompanying her to one friend's party. In other cases, although her family and friends liked the man, she complained that he was "not enough fun," or "didn't earn enough money." She constantly felt that if she "settled" now, she might lose out on the perfect soul mate or "ideal guy" later on.

When Betty came to therapy, one of her complaints was that she often thought she had met Mr. Right, but then started to see his negative qualities. As is common with persons who have a fear of commitment, Betty did not want to take the good with the bad. What she failed to realize was that no one is perfect, including herself. And, that people change as they get older. She agreed and told me about a guy she had dated for two years. In college, he had not appeared to be very strong and assertive, but now he had a high-powered job and was exactly her type. Eventually Betty began to have more realistic standards and started focusing on her dates' more lasting and important qualities when deciding whether or not to stay in the relationship.

LESSON: There is always something better. But you know what? You don't have *always*. If you keep up that mentality, you'll be searching for some nonexistent soul mate until the day you die. The only thing that matters is that the partner you are with makes you happy and comfortable. Don't compare him to outside standards. Only ask yourself "does he make me happy?" and "is he enough for me?" Don't compare him to the rest of the world—and don't compare him to your best friend's husband either.

Treating Your Fear of Commitment

In order to overcome your fear of commitment, you need to first accept the fact that no one is perfect. Here's a little exercise. Get out a piece of paper and make a list of your most undesirable qualities. Add physical ones if you must, but you should really focus on your habits, your ways of dealing with others, etc. Have you ever heard your friends or someone you date say, "I can't believe you're so X, Y, or Z?" Include that on the list. Now, take a look at your list. Are there qualities you'd like to change? Are there qualities that you've tried to change—say, for instance, you're messy and have tried to be neater—but it seems like you're stuck with them? Would you hope that, especially in the latter category, your ideal romantic partner would be able to accept these qualities about you?

Now, grab another piece of paper. Make a list of the last three guys you decided to stop seeing, then write down your reasoning for doing so. Were any of these qualities things they would have been willing—or capable—to change? Looking at them now, are these qualities that you could have lived with?

On the back side of that paper, or on another sheet, write down what your fears are when it comes to being in a relationship. Ask yourself if, realistically, the last three guys you dumped would have turned these fears into realities. You're asking yourself this because sometimes your fears can be so overpowering that you overestimate how damaging certain aspects of your relationship or even certain traits of your partner can really be to the overall relationship. You might see red flags where there really aren't any. In addition, if you're having trouble getting a date because you come across as a flight-risk or as someone who isn't able to commit, take a look at how these fears can be keeping you from even starting to get the life you want.

Depending on how intense your fear of commitment is, this exercise may have been enough to start to shake you out of the irrational thought patterns you've been letting control you. If not, consider sitting down with a counselor and asking them to help you address how realistic these issues are and have them help you work through them.

Signs you are progressing past your fear of commitment:

- You're willing to go out with someone for a third, fourth, or fifth date (base this on when you usually would bail).
- You're willing to accept at least one bad habit of your partner's.
- You've been dating someone for several months and not feeling critical towards them.
- You're okay thinking about future events and imagining your partner there with you.

SINGLE LADIES

If you have trouble getting a date, maybe you need to expand your zone of who is acceptable. You must be willing to date someone with different interests, educational level, or cultural background.

Fear of Vulnerability

If you were raised in an environment with people who could not be trusted or relied upon when you needed help, or if you were betrayed by a past lover, you may have developed a thick skin to prevent this type of hurt in the future. The problem with this is that the "thick skin" is a barrier to any close relationship, especially one with a lifetime partner. Persons may trick themselves into thinking that a fantasy soul mate would never betray them and would somehow never even make them fear betrayal, which would take away their fear of vulnerability. However, in the real world, a willingness to be vulnerable is a necessity for an intimate relationship. And while some men really *do* do things that can make you fear betrayal, loyalty isn't always as obvious. You can't question it constantly or ask your partner to prove his loyalty every hour. As long as he isn't doing anything to *provoke* your fears, you really just have to trust him.

Healthy relationships are built on communication and trust. When you can't permit yourself to trust your partner and allow yourself to be vulnerable in a romantic relationship, you make it that much more difficult to let someone get to know you and for you to truly feel fulfilled by a romantic relationship.

Signs you suffer from a fear of vulnerability:
- You resist sharing personal information for fear that it will give your partner something to hold over your head.
- You resist being close to or trusting others.
- You believe that people seeking an intimate relationship with you have ulterior motives.
- You believe that becoming close to someone makes you more susceptible to manipulation.

Where Does This Come From?

Clinical observation indicates that people who have a hard time letting their defenses down were likely emotionally or sexually taken advantage of in their youth—either by their family or their peers—or they witnessed those they cared about being taken advantage of. Children with a history of being shuffled among different caretakers often show fear of vulnerability.

Sometimes, the circumstances that caused this weren't quite so extreme; perhaps they weren't taken advantage of emotionally or sexually, but they experienced neglect by those they wanted to connect with closely. To protect themselves as adults, they keep an emotional distance from others so that if someone pulls away or neglects them, they don't feel the pain.

FEAR OF VULNERABILITY QUIZ

Take the following quiz to find out if you have a fear of vulnerability. As you take the quiz, be honest with yourself. If a statement applies to your life very often, circle 1. If it applies sometimes, circle 2. If it applies rarely, circle 3. And, if it never applies or applies only very rarely under certain circumstances, circle 4.

	OFTEN	SOMETIMES	RARELY	NEVER
If I disclose my fears to my partner, I fear that he will mock me.	1	2	3	4
I don't need to keep secrets from my partner.	1	2	3	4
Revealing personal information about myself gives the other person something to use against me.	1	2	3	4
I fight intimacy.	1	2	3	4
I believe people seeking intimacy have ulterior motives.	1	2	3	4
I seek out people from whom I can learn new things.	1	2	3	4

Scoring

For questions 1, 3, 4, and 5 give yourself one point for every 1, two points for every 2, three points for every 3, and four points for every 4. For the remaining questions, give yourself four points for every 1, three points for every 2, two points for every 3, and one point for every 4.

Interpretation

Add your points for questions 1 through 6. If your score is 6 to 12, you have a significant fear of vulnerability. If your score is 13 to 18, your fear of vulnerability is within the average range. If your score is 19 to 24, you have no real fear of vulnerability.

SOUL MATE SCENARIOS:
Heather

In the past, someone Heather loved had hurt her emotionally. As a result she started to judge people before she knew them, using what she thought was her profound intuition. She thought that the way one person behaved served as a general rule for how all people would behave. On top of that, she believed that she understood how all men felt and behaved and thought it was unwise to trust them.

Unfortunately for Heather, this eventually backfired when she met a guy who was very patient with her and her closed-off nature. But, she was scared of opening up to him because she worried that she would sound like she had baggage and she didn't want to lose him.

In order to help Heather move past her fear of vulnerability, she had to first dispute her irrational belief that all men were not to be trusted. She compared (and, more important, contrasted) her present—this new guy and their dynamic—with the bad experiences of the past so she could see the difference. In doing so, I gently reminded her that by talking to me she shared information without negative consequences. I encouraged her to start to share some little things with this new guy. She started by telling him about some of her strange tastes in food, like enjoying pickles with chocolate syrup. Sure, he made a grossed-out face, but he also told her he thought it was cute and that in fact he sometimes ate his dog's biscuits. The two had a good laugh over it and it ended up bringing them closer together. And, because she received this generally positive reaction instead of the negative one she had expected, she started opening up and sharing more with him.

LESSON: You cannot allow the actions of one man dictate the way you feel about all men. Even though it is scary, you need to give new people a chance to show you that they are open to who you are. After all, the most satisfying relationship that you can have is the one in which you're able to show all if not most of yourself. In order to have that relationship, you're going to have to make yourself vulnerable and take the risk of possibly being ridiculed. But when you find the guy who accepts you—even knowing all your quirks—then you've found a good match.

Treating Your Fear of Vulnerability

Hate to break it to you, but dealing with your fears is going to involve being a little, well, scared sometimes. It's going to mean doing the thing that scares you so you can realize that it's really not all that scary in the first place. To deal with your fears of vulnerability, you need to start putting yourself through *systematic desensitization* with your partner. The idea behind systematic desensitization is that the more you experience something, the less you feel the effects of it. In this case, you start sharing little things and see how the guy you're dating or interested in reacts. To break the ice, ask your guy a question like, "What are five things I don't know about you?" You then have to answer the question in return. Some of these questions can be silly, some of them can be more serious, this way, both of you are vulnerable and you're not just sitting there bearing your heart to a stone wall. It also puts less gravity on what you are sharing. Of course you want your guy to take you seriously, but if you sit someone down and say, "We need to have a talk," and you list off every weird thing you think he should know about you, it might make it seem like those things are actually *more* of a problem than they really are. The less weight you put on the things you share with him, the less weight he will put on them too. If there are big things in your past that you don't want to address, don't feel like you have to share everything in this one exercise.

Now there is always a chance that the person might react poorly, but that is something you need to figure out. If you share something personal with a guy and he reacts in a negative way, he probably isn't someone you want to be with anyway. But hopefully this exercise will actually help you see that they are someone you can trust and with whom you can share those bigger issues with later.

When it comes to those bigger issues, remember, the longer you hold your feelings inside the longer they start to eat away at you. They are most likely affecting your behavior and hindering you from being as happy as you could be. When you can let them out into the open and share them with a partner, you can begin to work through them.

Signs that you're progressing past your fear of vulnerability:
- You're ready to reveal a secret or two to a close friend.
- You're ready to reveal some of your less pretty emotions to the person you're dating.
- You feel comfortable and trusting around your partner because you no longer believe that they will emotionally hurt you.

Fear of Abandonment

In good relationships, there is a balance of togetherness and separateness where each partner maintains their individuality and identity and uses them to enrich the relationship, rather than suffocating or keeping their partner at a distance. But, if you have a fear of abandonment, you might need too much from your partner and, as a result, end up pushing them away.

Signs you suffer from a fear of abandonment:

- You have a tendency to cling to your partner or others in your life.
- You show excessive concern about the people in your life and possibly even anger or jealousy in the hope of gaining attention or acknowledgment.
- You do the opposite—you often pick fights or consciously run away from love.

Where Does This Come From?

In many cases where people have a fear of abandonment, someone they cared about exited their life abruptly. Sometimes this is dealt with in a healthy way, sometimes a person who has experienced this suffers from a fear of vulnerability, and sometimes it results in a fear of abandonment. Often, the person who is left behind blames herself and wants to prevent it from happening again. Unfortunately, this fear may become a self-fulfilling prophecy if she holds on so tightly that her partner becomes angry and distant and wants to get away for fear of suffocation.

FEAR OF ABANDONMENT QUIZ

Take the following quiz to find out if you have a fear of abandonment. As you take the quiz, be honest with yourself. If a statement applies to your life very often, circle 1. If it applies sometimes, circle 2. If it applies rarely, circle 3. And, if it never applies or applies only very rarely under certain circumstances, circle 4.

	OFTEN	SOMETIMES	RARELY	NEVER
When my partner is away, I fear that something terrible has happened to him.	1	2	3	4
I trust my partner to be faithful to me when I am not around.	1	2	3	4
Forming close relationships is important to me.	1	2	3	4
I would not approach a man who was very handsome.	1	2	3	4
I feel overwhelmed when I am in an intimate relationship.	1	2	3	4
People in close relationships tend to lose their own identities.	1	2	3	4

Scoring

For questions 1, 4, 5, and 6 give yourself one point for every 1, two points for every 2, three points for every 3, and four points for every 4. For the remaining questions, give yourself four points for every 1, three points for every 2, two points for every 3, and one point for every 4.

Interpretation

Add your points for questions 1 through 6. If your score is 6 to 12, you have a significant fear of abandonment, if your score is 13 to 18, your fear of abandonment is within the average range. If your score is 19 to 24, you have no real fear of abandonment.

SOUL MATE SCENARIOS: *Jennifer*

Jennifer and Brian had been dating for several months when they decided to move in together. Jennifer suddenly became concerned when Brian went out with friends. What was he doing? Why did he need to go out with the boys? Was he seeing another girl? Jennifer constantly texted him while he was out with friends or when he was at work. In several incidents, when Brian did not respond quickly enough to her text, Jennifer showed up at the bar, his friend's house, or his place of work. Eventually, Brian had had enough and said that he wanted to move out. Jennifer threw a tantrum, began throwing his possessions around the room, saying she knew Brian was cheating on her. Brian packed his possessions and left. He had not been cheating, but he could no longer live with Jennifer's constant accusations and badgering. As Jennifer watched him walk away she felt devastated because she had created what she most feared—the love of her life leaving her.

LESSON: It is your responsibility to treat your fears so your partner can be himself without having to worry about provoking them. There was very little Brian could have done to make Jennifer's fears go away, because he was not doing anything wrong. If you are aware of certain fears you have, when you feel them taking over, stop and analyze the situation. Ask yourself, "Has my partner *really* done something to provoke this?" You could save yourself from pushing away a great partner.

Treating Your Fear of Abandonment

The first step in treating your fear of abandonment is for you to realize that if you suffocate a loved one, they will likely start to develop a realistic fear of engulfment about being in a relationship with you. At some point, if fear of abandonment seems to have been the cause of past breakups, it may be important to seek counseling to deal with these issues before you enter another serious relationship; sometimes the circumstances involving family and past relationships were quite traumatic and difficult to deal with, and require the help of an objective source such as a counselor. If you do have a fear of abandonment, instead of facing the issue and trying to work through it, you may just tell yourself that one man—your soul mate—will come along who will behave so perfectly that you will never have cause to fear abandonment. But that person is never going to come along because your fears will cause you to perceive any man's behavior through the lens of that fear. And you could constantly sabotage a great relationship.

Signs that you are progressing past your fear of abandonment:
- You no longer text or call your partner when he's out with his friends or question him about where he's been when he returns.
- You are able to be happy when your partner is not with you.
- You trust that your partner will be faithful even when you are unaware of his whereabouts.

Fear of Rejection

The soul mate myth is a powerful fantasy for women who fear rejection. Imaginary lovers never reject you because they know all of your inner workings, your hopes and dreams, without you even sharing these with them. They are constantly enthusiastic about your goals—they are your personal cheerleader and you never once have to even ask for that support. This is important because when women fear rejection, they will often buy into this myth and allow themselves to be quiet in their relationships. They allow themselves to not speak up about their dreams, aspirations, ups and downs, and overall personal lives. They fear a man won't want to hear about all this, that it will drag him down or bore him, so they hold on to the idea that if this man is their soul mate, he will show enthusiasm for their life all on his own, without her ever bringing it up. Women often step into the role of superwoman; we listen to and support our man's hopes and dreams and take care of him when he is sick, but don't expect the same in return. But your partner should be impressed if you tell him about your career goals, he should sympathize with you if you've had a hard day at work, he should celebrate with you if you get a promotion. But you have to *tell* him these things. He'll want to hear them. And if he doesn't, isn't that good for you to know? Then you can move on to the next guy that will want to hear about your life.

Signs you have a fear of rejection:

- You believe that if you revealed your true self, your partner would reject or ridicule you.
- You don't tell your partner when he has hurt your feelings because you don't want him to become aggravated that you're starting conflict.
- You constantly worry that your partner misinterpreted something you did or said.
- You are afraid you might not live up to your partner's standards.

Where Does This Come From?

Often people who have been humiliated for expressing opinions that were different from their family or peers develop a belief that if they reveal their true selves, they will not be liked. If, for example, your parents held certain political or religious views and you were not allowed to express your views if they differed, you may be conditioned to believe that voicing your opinion or needs will always result in conflict, or that you won't be listened to at all. What results is a generalized fear of revealing anything other than superficial likes, dislikes, and discussion of topics that will not provoke conflict. But your partner isn't someone you're just sharing an elevator with for a brief moment. He is the person you are supposed to be intimate with. He is the person with whom, after a long day where you had to be politically correct and diplomatic with everyone you met, you can just let loose, stop trying to save face, and just be yourself.

FEAR OF REJECTION QUIZ

Take the following quiz to find out if you have a fear of rejection. As you take the quiz, be honest with yourself. If a statement applies to your life very often, circle 1. If it applies sometimes, circle 2. If it applies rarely, circle 3. And, if it never applies or applies only very rarely under certain circumstances, circle 4.

	OFTEN	SOMETIMES	RARELY	NEVER
I am better off keeping my opinions to myself because my partner will probably think they are stupid.	1	2	3	4
I avoid having arguments when I'm in a relationship because I think my partner will feel like I am wasting his time by arguing.	1	2	3	4
I can approach a man if I find him attractive.	1	2	3	4
When my partner is unavailable I fear that he is cheating on me.	1	2	3	4
I find it difficult to be alone.	1	2	3	4
I am willing to make compromises that go against my personal beliefs to remain in an intimate relationship.	1	2	3	4

Scoring

For questions 1, 2, 4, 5, and 6 give yourself one point for every 1, two points for every 2, three points for every 3, and four points for every 4. For the remaining question, give yourself four points for a 1, three points for a 2, two points for a 3, and one point for a 4.

Interpretation

Add your points for questions 1 through 6. If your score is 6 to 12, you have a significant fear of rejection. If your score is 13 to 18, your fear of rejection is within the average range. If you scored 19 to 24, you have no real fear of rejection.

SOUL MATE SCENARIOS:
Suzanne

Suzanne's friend suggested that she go on a blind date with Kevin. Suzanne heard that he was a lawyer and quite handsome but started to fear that she was not educated enough or pretty enough for him and started to regret agreeing to go on the date. But, at her friend's urging, she went anyway. During the date, Kevin seemed attracted to Suzanne and a few days later, he called her for a second date. Fearing that Kevin would eventually find her dull and unattractive she turned him down. Suzanne preferred talking to people on the Internet, not meeting them, and fantasizing about them instead.

LESSON: Like Suzanne, your fear of rejection could be keeping you from quality relationships or at the very least, great dates. Stop setting yourself up for failure and stop allowing your fears to dictate which sorts of experiences you allow yourself to have.

Treating Your Fear of Rejection

One of the methods I use when working with people who have fear of rejection are having them do *risk exercises*. I actually suggest that they go out there and try to get rejected or ridiculed. By doing this purposely, they become desensitized to negative reaction from others. They also learn to laugh at themselves; and a sense of humor is a highly desirable trait in women as well as men. In doing these exercises as games, I've had women go on the New York City subway with a plant with condoms on it and a sign that reads "This is a rubber plant." I've assigned women to walk a banana as if it were a dog. Sure they're silly, but they also get people to confront their fears. Others will laugh or look at them funny, but then they start to realize it's not that bad. Think of the craziest thing you've seen someone do. Did you actually stop and point at them and ridicule them? Probably not, because people rarely do that. Everyone has their own behavior that is a little odd or even seemingly crazy, but the good news is, everyone knows that everyone has that kind of behavior. You're not going to be singled out for having a few quirks or flaws.

Fear of Novelty

Most of us like a reference point. We like to be able to compare a person or a situation to one we have already experienced because it gives us the sense that we know what to expect. People with a true fear of novelty, a fear of something new, avoid all situations and people that are entirely unfamiliar because they are afraid of not knowing what to expect. But the truth is, you can never really know what to expect from someone, even if they remind you of someone you know very well. Many people who buy into the soul mate myth have a fear of novelty, and they like the idea of a soul mate who would never push them out of their comfort zone—someone who feels entirely familiar. They believe that their soul mate must be someone who shares their same interests, desires, and needs. While a certain degree of commonality can help with compatibility, if you're looking for someone who is just like you, you're closing yourself off to a lot of great potential matches. And, sometimes, it can keep you in stagnant or harmful relationships when you could be out there finding the man of your dreams.

Signs you have a fear of novelty:
- You do not consider partners who have different backgrounds than you.
- You tend to fear change or new experiences.

- You stay in relationships even when you know they're going nowhere or are harmful to your physical being or self-esteem.

Where Does This Come From?

If you had a family that encouraged you to "stick with your own kind" and was openly rejecting of anyone different, you may have difficulty accepting people who are different from you ethnically, culturally, or in any other way. You may prefer to stick with the tried and true, which, of course only serves to narrow your opportunities. In the case of dating or a relationship, this can make you nervous to step away from a relationship that you're used to, even if it isn't good for you.

You also could be intimidated by the prospect of trying to understand someone who has many obvious different qualities than yourself because you do not know what comes along with that territory—you know what behaviors to expect from people with similar qualities to yourself. But the truth is, plenty of guys could write you off because you have a certain quality that is foreign to them, and they might be guys who *you* were interested in. Try to remember that there isn't always safety in the familiar, and there isn't always danger in exploring someone new.

FEAR OF NOVELTY QUIZ

Take the following quiz to find out if you have a fear of novelty. As you take the quiz, be honest with yourself. If a statement applies to your life very often, circle 1. If it applies sometimes, circle 2. If it applies rarely, circle 3. And, if it never applies or applies only very rarely under certain circumstances, circle 4.

	OFTEN	SOMETIMES	RARELY	NEVER
I avoid dating men who are not of a similar cultural background.	1	2	3	4
I don't like to venture into unfamiliar territory.	1	2	3	4
I am happy to try new activities suggested by my partner.	1	2	3	4
Predictability is a very important trait in a man.	1	2	3	4
I don't like it when my partner spends too much time with others.	1	2	3	4
If my partner suggests a new activity, I become a bit anxious.	1	2	3	4

Scoring

For questions 1, 2, 4, 5, and 6 give yourself one point for every 1, two points for every 2, three points for every 3, and four points for every 4. For the remaining question, give yourself four points for a 1, three points for a 2, two points for a 3, and one point for a 4.

Interpretation

Add your points for questions 1 through 6. If your score is 6 to 12, you have a significant fear of novelty. If your score is 13 to 18, your fear of novelty is within the average range. If your score is 19 to 24, you have no significant fear of novelty.

SOUL MATE SCENARIOS:
Roseanne

Roseanne and Vinny had been dating for three years. They were in their twenties and both held good jobs and had discussed getting engaged, but, Vinny was just not a nice guy. Often Roseanne worked hard to do things "just right" to avoid Vinny's criticisms and other nasty comments because she was afraid to be alone and was scared that she'd never meet anyone else who would tell her that he loved her.

One day Roseanne was offered a promotion at work, but she needed to prepare answers for an interview before the job promotion could be finalized. She asked Vinny if she could run her answers by him before the interview for practice. He constantly interrupted her and criticized her answers, and when it came time for the interview, Roseanne felt so insecure because of Vinny's criticisms, that she actually failed the interview and didn't get the job. She finally decided to leave Vinny, realizing that his criticisms were affecting more than just her love life and that it was actually better to be alone than to be in a relationship that was detrimental to other parts of her life.

LESSON: The status quo is not necessarily the best way. Particularly for women who marry young or who have not had many partners, it can be easy to think "this might be as good as it gets." But honestly, it's not. If your partner is being cruel or condescending to you, that's not good, let alone as good as it gets. In that situation you are better off being on your own or braving it to see who else is out there instead of just remaining in the relationship because it is familiar.

Treating Your Fear of Novelty

Granted, your situation might not be as extreme as Roseanne's. Maybe you just stay in relationships even after you've realized that they're not working and that no matter how much you care for the other person, you two aren't going to be able to solve your issues. It's sad when two people who love each other are romantically incompatible, but by letting go, you can find someone with whom you are truly romantically compatible. If you buy into the soul mate myth, you may think that when you're with the "perfect" man, you won't experience any fear—nothing will seem unfamiliar about him and you won't be pushed out of your comfort zone. But there is always a risk in getting involved with someone new, and you never know what you'll discover when you explore a new person. There will always be some element of fear in that, but if you're going to find a quality relationship, you have to push through that fear.

If you're not sure what to do in your relationship, try creating a payoff matrix. This involves looking at the gains and losses from all sides. To do this take a piece of paper and make two columns. On one side, write "being single." On the other, write "staying with the person I'm with." List the pros and cons for both. Which pros are more worthwhile? Which cons can you not live with? You'll probably have your answer on what to do.

Signs that you're progressing past your fear of novelty:

- You try a new activity even if you were initially uncomfortable.
- You date someone who is different from who you usually go out with.
- You date someone who is of a group, or type, you were previously uncomfortable with.
- You leave the man you're with because you realize he's not good for your self-esteem.

Forget Fear

In this section you learned to recognize and face down your fears related to not finding a perfect match or being rejected by someone you care about. You learned that since a true soul mate is pure fantasy, there is no such thing as a man who will magically not provoke any of your fears. So long as you don't address your fears and hopefully rid yourself of them, any man you get involved with will bring those fears out. The sooner you address and overcome your fears, the sooner you make yourself available to experience new men and actually get to know them with nothing holding you back.

Soul Mate Summary

This may have been a hard chapter to read, but hopefully it's helped you identify the barriers that may have stopped you on your road to true romance. Over
time—and with therapy if necessary—it's possible for you to overcome these
walls. The sooner you do, the quicker you'll be ready to meet someone who
could be your lifelong partner. As you work towards banishing fear from your
life—and loves—keep the following in mind:

- If you have any major relationship fears that are doing you a dis-
  service in love, you must learn to recognize these fears before you
  can find good love.

- There are six common fears that get in the way of pursuing a good
  love relationship. These are fear of engulfment, fear of commitment, fear of vulnerability, fear of abandonment, fear of rejection,
  and fear of novelty.

- Cognitive behavioral therapy (CBT), which is based on the premise
  that intense negative feelings—for example, fear, anger, guilt, and
  depression—result from irrational beliefs, can help you deal with
  those common fears and help you kick the soul mate myth to the
  curb.

- There are specific statements that constitute irrational beliefs; and
  you can learn to dispute those irrational beliefs that create barriers
  in relationships.

- You can identify signs that you are progressing past your fears and
  are on the road to healthy attitudes and positive relationships.

. . . .

REWIRING YOUR BRAIN:
Teaching Yourself How to Love

Let out a sigh of relief because the hardest part is over—the part where you admit that you're afraid of a thing or two and that some of your expectations may not be completely realistic. The good thing is that you're not alone, no one's perfect, and a lot of women struggle with the very issues you identified in Step 1. But now it's time to take the next step and train yourself to recognize and find real love.

In this part, you will learn to identify the factors that are important in a good relationship, you'll practice letting go of your unrealistic expectations, and you'll learn to recognize the difference between reasonable and unreasonable expectations for a partner. You'll also have one last chance to grieve for that mythic man you couldn't find. Then you'll then be ready to face the future, unencumbered by the fantasy of finding a soul mate. It'll be great, once you get there, so read on!

CHAPTER 4

Letting Go a Little

Before you can move forward towards meeting a great guy there are some things that you need to let go of. It's perfectly fine to desire your partner to have similar interests as you, or to have certain abilities, or to even look a certain way, but that perfect soul mate doesn't exist and you need to stop being blinded by your search for those particular qualities and not noticing a man's own unique but wonderful traits when they are right in front of you, just because he doesn't meet the other "requirements." Don't worry though, letting go of some of your expectations isn't as hard as you may think. And the good news is that there are things that you *do* get to hold on to: attraction and compatibility. You just have to learn to reconsider what qualities lead to these things in a relationship.

Constructing the Perfect Man—on Paper

Look, it's okay to have a general idea of what kind of man you want to be involved with. You'd like him to be funny, warm-hearted, emotionally stable, and emotionally intelligent. Great! But, be honest, do you want all of the above *plus* he has to be tall, commit two hours a day to his fitness, be well-off, drive a nice car, etc.? If you say, "I *just* want a good guy" but then you also require all of those subsequent particular qualities, then you are lying to yourself. You don't *just* want a good guy. You're pickier than you realize.

The problem with a list like this is that you might miss out on a Mr. Right-for-You because you're out there looking for your soul mate, who isn't going to show up. Now, no one is saying that you won't end up with a sweet, attractive, romantic guy who is tall and has a good job, but when you start getting really specific you start closing off doors. Remember when we discussed mental filtering, focusing upon one aspect of a situation, rather than seeing the whole picture, in Chapter 3? Having a list that's too specific is like that.

The real danger is that while some characteristics, such as your physical attraction to someone, may be evident from the start, other traits may take some time to reveal themselves. People are complex creatures, and as a result, most of us don't show all our traits at once. Do you walk into a party and immediately reveal that you are not only intelligent, funny, and ambitious, but that you love to cuddle in bed and are the type to surprise your lover with sexy lingerie from time to time? Didn't think so.

So, let's say you meet a man who seems laid back and a little shy. He doesn't kiss you on the first date. Maybe not even the second. So, you categorize him as wimpy or not very manly and you decide to not see him again because on that list of mandatory requirements is "strong man." But, had you stuck around, you would have discovered this guy was the type who lets the little things roll off his back and that respecting a woman was extremely important to him. You'd have realized that once you gave him the green light, he would actually blow your mind in bed or you might have discovered that even though he hadn't fit into the corporate world, he actually was a creative entrepreneur with a burgeoning business of his own that left him time to spend with you. Oops is right!

The lesson here is that you shouldn't judge anyone by what they do—or don't do—on your first or second meeting. There could be a lot of great things under the surface.

But He's Just My Type!

Do you have a type? A typical guy that you fall for? Do you only date tall, dark, and handsome men? Blonde, blue-eyed, guys who look good in a suit? Men who have a PhD or earn over $100,000 per year? You have to get past this tunnel vision!

There are two very big problems with only being willing to date within your type. The first is that you're of course shutting yourself off from meeting lots of great men based on a set of arbitrary characteristics. The second problem is that whether you're attracted to a certain personality type or a certain appearance type, that kind of person may not be good for you. There may be a *reason* your relationships continue to not work out or to not even materialize at all. Maybe you like the outdoors but continue to look for men in bars. If you like the outdoors, the best place to meet a man with similar interests is *outdoors,* not in bars. Maybe you like guys who have an "edge." They're pierced, tattooed, and have that cool James Dean–like attitude. And then you find out they all have issues with authority or with staying faithful, etc. Or maybe you like handsome men who turn out to have intense narcissistic tendencies. You'd like for them to see your point of view but they've gotten it in their head that their beauty is a gift to women and think you can just be replaced. Now, of course, not all men who fit those visual descriptions act like that. You can't judge a book by its cover . . . and that's exactly the point. The lesson here is that you don't have to play against your type, but be open to others. If you feel an initial attraction, you might find that what lies underneath will surprise you.

SOUL MATE SCENARIOS:
Grace

Grace had been dating Kevin for a few years before she was hired to work for a production company. She was suddenly going to glamorous, exciting events on a weekly basis and meeting impressive, even famous individuals. Everyone around her discussed things like up-and-coming independent film makers and new art exhibits. She had always been very happy with Kevin who was a mechanical engineer. His life was not glamorous at all, but his job was stable, he was home every night to be with her and he treated her kindly. However, with her new job, Grace began to wish Kevin had more of an interest in the types of things that she discussed with her coworkers. She started to feel her life was too different and fast-moving for Kevin and she broke up with him. However, after a few months spent going on dates with men in her industry, she began to realize a lot of them had philandering tendencies and were rather pretentious. Yes, they could discuss all of the things Grace found so intriguing, but they didn't make good partners. Looking back, she realized she didn't *need* a man that lead this fast life like she did. She just *wanted* one. What she needed was someone faithful and caring. And she had walked away from that with Kevin because she mistook her want for a need.

LESSON: Sometimes *all* of your needs cannot be met by one relationship. You may be able to have stimulating conversations about work with your colleagues that you cannot have with your partner, but you need to consider what is really important in a *romantic* relationship. When you're sick, when you need someone to cheer you up, or when you have kids, will you really care that your partner can't talk extensively about what you do for a living? Meanwhile you can find that connection through other relationships—like with friends or coworkers—without having to end your romantic one.

REASONABLE NEEDS

Everyone has their own deal-breakers, but here are a few needs you shouldn't be willing to budge on.

- Respect
- Same definition of fidelity
- Sexual attraction
- Emotional availability (He shouldn't be married or in a committed relationship.)
- Equal balance of power (More importance isn't put on one or the other's career, personal troubles, family, obligations etc. You discuss decisions that affect the both of you.)
- Trustworthiness
- Openness and vulnerability
- Concern for your well-being

EXERCISE: WANTS AND NEEDS

Before we go any further, take a few minutes to lay out your wants and needs so you know where you're starting from. Grab a piece of paper and make three columns. On the top of the first, write the word "Need." On the top of the second, write, "Want," and on the top of the third, write, "Undecided." Now, write down whatever characteristics you feel are important into the categories in which you feel they belong. Put any you can't decide between wanting and needing into the undecided column. If you're not sure how to fill out your columns see the table below for inspiration:

NEED	WANT	UNDECIDED
Faithful	Good in bed	College Degree
Employed	Rich	Same religion
Wants Kids	Handsome	Lives within an hour's drive
Has similar long-term goals	Funny	Helps with household chores

Are you having trouble differentiating between a want and a need? There are probably things you think you *need* in a man, where in fact you just really *want* them.

You'll recognize the things you *need* as the things that, if they are lacking, are a constant cause for conflict in your relationship. Most fights stem back to the fact that the man is missing that trait. But if a man is missing the things you simply *want* this won't really cause tension. You're not going to fight because your boyfriend doesn't have the exact career you wanted him to have. You are going to fight, however, if he doesn't have a job, doesn't make an effort to get one, and you're constantly stuck paying his bills. See the difference? There are likely some things you want your man to have, but, if he doesn't have them it's not a complete deal-breaker. Your relationship wouldn't *die* without them.

Now, look at those columns you filled out. Think of the items in the need column as deal-breakers. Without them, you couldn't be in the relationship. Think of the items in your want column as characteristics you would prefer your partner to have but if they don't have them you could still be happy in the relationship. Take a moment to consider this and, if you need to, move some of those *need* traits into the *want* column. Many women break off relationships because they mistake the qualities they want in a man for ones they need, and when they look back they realize he actually did possess the traits she needed, and that those are harder to find than the superficial traits that she left him for not having.

Living Outside the List

We've just addressed how confusing your wants for needs, or having even irrational needs or wants, could be getting you into trouble. Now, let's take a look at some of the common needs and wants that show up on these lists and how to start climbing over those artificial barriers to finding your Mr. Right.

The Physical Characteristic Barrier

You already know you have a type or types, and you probably recognize that this type is determined by your previous behavior. Who you admired growing up, your first boyfriend, your first love, all influenced your current type. But, this conditioned reflex can be altered. Just take a look at Kathy. . . .

SOUL MATE SCENARIOS:
Kathy

Kathy had been married to Michael for ten years. He had dark hair, dark eyes, and a mustache. But, after a painful divorce, she found herself single. When she was ready to start dating again, a friend of hers set her up on a blind date with Gary. Expecting her friend knew what her "type" was, she was shocked to discover that Gary was a redhead. But as the pair talked through dinner, she discovered that she had far more in common with Gary when it came to interests, feelings, and values than she ever had with Michael and she agreed to go on a second date with him. After that promising first date, she started to notice more and more redheaded guys and found that "type" more attractive.

LESSON: You were not born with a type. Instead, your vision of the perfect man was created through a series of positive experiences with that type. And, just as you were able to grow an attraction for one type of man by giving him a chance and allowing him to reveal all his sides to you, you can grow that attraction with other types of men. Also, consider this: if your relationships haven't been working out with guys who are your "type," then maybe that sort of guy isn't your type after all.

Your Homework

You guessed it: I want you to intentionally go on dates with someone who is a different physical type than you're usually attracted to. Try going on one of these dates once a week if you can. Don't go out with someone you find ugly, but find someone you find yourself at least mildly attracted to and go for it. If you find that you like your date as a person, you may even start to think that type is handsome!

SINGLE LADIES

If you are having difficulty meeting men to date, it is important to expand your circle of friends, interests, activities, and expectations. You may think physical attraction is a simple thing—that you find someone attractive because they just *are*. But guess what? There is a lot more going on than just the symmetry of his face, his physique, or even his clothes when it comes to attraction. Without knowing it, you've categorized people. Maybe you loved a tan, blonde man once before. So when you see a tan, blonde man today, a dozen silent memos go off in your head, like "he is funny, sweet, adventurous, etc." But there is actually very little about some-one's physical appearance that can serve as an indicator of their character. Your best bet if you're trying to date outside your box is to tell yourself you know *nothing* about a person just by looking at him. So go learn about him.

The Cultural Barrier

Though similar to the physical barrier, this barrier has more to do with your ethnicity or the culture that you grew up in. Let's say you were raised in a household where the only acceptable men to date were those of the same ethnicity or cultural background. It's possible that you've never branched out of this original constraint. For some, this cultural barrier is erected because you know your family would be disappointed if you stepped outside of your culture and for some it's because it would feel out of the norm to you.

Still, every day, I see happy couples of two different faiths, two different ethnicities, and two different cultural backgrounds. Don't let your past prejudices stand in the way of true love.

SOUL MATE SCENARIOS:
Tara

Growing up, Tara was raised in an Italian household and her parents impressed upon her that she needed to date "nice Italian guys." She tried, but by the time she started medical school she still hadn't met one with whom she really clicked. While she was in school she discovered that the student population was very diverse and while there she met an Indian guy named Tom. Tara and Tom had a lot in common. When she first met his parents she was a little worried that they wouldn't accept her because of their different family backgrounds, but they made her feel right at home. Tara's family was initially more difficult. They acted somewhat cool when they first met Tom. He was not surprised, as Tara had warned him about their narrow-mindedness. However, as her family observed how well Tom treated Tara, and got to know him as a person, they began to accept him as a welcome friend of the family. In fact, Tara, and Tom are now engaged!

LESSON: In most cases where parents have specific qualifications for the partners of their children, the parents only set those parameters because they believe their children will be happiest with partners who meet those qualifications. In other words, they *just* want you to be happy. And if you find a different way to be happy, with a different person than they had imagined, they will usually accept that partner so long as they see you smiling.

Your Homework

If you have a fear of being an outsider, you may not like this assignment. But now's the time to join a club or group in your town that focuses on a certain culture like a French conversation group, an African American studies group, a class that learns only Indian cooking, and so on. You may be the *only* person there that is not originally from the focused-on culture, but this will accomplish two positive things: 1) you will get to know a large group of people from a certain culture in a more natural context. Unlike being on a date when the spotlight is on, no one is the center of attention in a group like this and you can just realize that you can have plenty in common with people of an entirely different background from yours. And, 2) you might meet a man there who really appreciates the fact that you aren't afraid to put yourself in new situations and learn about different kinds of people. No one can predict the future, but opening yourself up to new experiences can sometimes have a profoundly positive effect on your life.

SINGLE LADIES

If you have difficulty getting dates because you feel shy and afraid of rejection, try to approach three men each week whom you like, but feel intimidated by because you think they're too smart, too handsome, too popular, or too confident. The exercise requires that you not expect a positive response, but make a simple approach such as asking how to use an exercise machine at the gym. Usually at least one of the men is interested and will want to get to know you better—and there's nothing wrong with that!

The Age Barrier

Alright, so you've opened yourself up to the idea that maybe you could fall in love with someone who doesn't look the way you originally envisioned your ideal man. But what about age? Isn't it important that the person you choose to spend your life with be of a similar age and at a similar stage in life? Wouldn't someone much older than you be a fuddy-duddy, and don't guys who are much younger than you not know what they want? Well, that *can* be the case, but there are some men who are very young at heart even though they might be as many as twenty years older than you, and some very mature guys who could be up to twenty years younger than you. The important thing is that you've reached the same level of maturity, and this usually comes from having experienced many of the same things. The good news is that you can usually deduce what someone's maturity level will be by learning about their life experiences—there is a difference between a twenty-five-year-old who is still finishing college, and a twenty-five-year-old who is a successful entrepreneur, after all.

One advantage to dating younger men is that women in their thirties have a sex drive that is closer to that of men in their twenties than that of men their same age. That's because men hit their sexual peak around the age of eighteen and women hit theirs around thirty-five. Another advantage is that younger men are pretty energetic and will want to experience things that an older man may have no interest in because he has already been there. In addition, younger men—if they are mature—will also admire your wisdom and will feel lucky to be with a woman who already knows how to treat a man and be a good partner.

On the other side, older men are more likely to understand what it means to be a gentleman and are often more willing and able to give financially as well as emotionally, since they are more established in their careers and in their emotional life. Older men have also already been through the experimentation phase, and are usually more likely to be ready to settle down. And, unlike younger men who may still be figuring out what they're looking for in a partner and in the bedroom, older men don't tend to wander away from a woman after they've been pleased sexually. Not to mention the fact that they are usually—let's face it—better in bed because they have more experience. The reality is, they've probably had enough sexual partners in their lifetime by now to realize that the thrill of a new sexual conquest gets old, and eventually companionship is what you can actually enjoy day in and day out. However, it's important to keep in mind that these scenarios are just suppositions and you have to keep your eyes—and your heart—open to any guy who might be right for you regardless of age.

SOUL MATE SCENARIOS:
Karen

Karen, who was in her mid-twenties, had always been very mature for her age and took on a lot of responsibilities at a young age, starting her own company at the age of twenty-two. While most of her friends had 9 to 5 jobs, went out and partied every night, and were happy with just casual dates or flings, Karen's career came along with a whole different set of desires for her personal life. She had to work nights and weekends. She was usually preoccupied thinking about her career even when she was convinced to go out socially. She needed someone who she could run her ideas for her business by and she needed a lot of emotional support because running her own business was very taxing. She met Ben, who was in his early forties, on an online dating site. Ben had a business of his own, as well, and had been established in it for over fifteen years. He proved to be not only very attractive to Karen, but was also a great mentor, who was able to offer her tremendous business advice and was enthusiastic to listen to her ideas. Since he was a little older, he was over the party scene as well, and was happy to just relax with Karen on her nights when she didn't work.

LESSON: Just because someone doesn't come from your generation or isn't right near your same age, that doesn't mean they wouldn't be a great partner.

Your Homework

Age really is just a number. It's the personality of the guy that you should focus on. Many times a person has much in common with you regardless of their chronological age. If they display the most important traits, such as honesty, loyalty, kindness, faithfulness, and a supportive personality, this outweighs the age factor. Dating someone younger could be kind of fun and may turn into the committed relationship that is just right for both of you. Or, if you try the reverse, you might find you have discovered someone who has the emotional maturity and intellect you've been trying to find in men your own age. The important thing is that you feel that the two of you are equals and you treat each other as such. If you're attracted to an older man, but you feel like he is just looking for a cute, young plaything—probably not the best match. But if the man speaks to you with respect and appreciates your opinions, your respective ages really shouldn't matter.

The Introvert/Extrovert Barrier

Would you prefer to be the life of the party, or the woman chatting up one friend at a time? Just because a man is an introvert —or an extrovert—and you're not, doesn't mean that you two can't be a good match. In this case, it all comes down to respecting each other's boundaries and allowing the other person to be themselves. And, keep in mind, people reveal different sides to their personality given the setting. At a party filled with all of his friends, your man might be the loudest, funniest guy in the room, whereas if he's attending a gallery event with you, he might be more reserved in order to be respectful.

SOUL MATE SCENARIOS:
Harold

Harold was a drill sergeant who was usually attracted to intellectual, more liberal-minded women who weren't involved in the military. But he sometimes had a hard time attracting these kinds of women because when he wasn't working, he was shy and didn't know how to dress the part to attract those women.

But, then, he met Sandy. She was bright, chatty, and appreciated the liberal viewpoint. From their first meeting, she and Harold had great chemistry and the pair claim that when they saw each other it was pretty much love at first sight. In fact, Sandy didn't even notice that Harold was a poor dresser or that he was somewhat reserved because she loved him for who he was and this brought out the best in him. Pretty quickly, as he became more comfortable with Sandy—and with himself—Harold started to be interested in dressing better, became a great conversationalist, and even turned into somewhat of a social butterfly!

LESSON: If you click with someone who seems very different from you, explore that chemistry. You could bring out the best in each other because you are drawn to the qualities in one another that you would like to cultivate in yourselves.

Your Homework

When you go out with a man who is not "your type," don't tiptoe around your differences and behave in a way that you think will make him most comfortable. Treat him the way you would treat a guy who has the qualities you usually go for. After a few dates, you may notice that these qualities are all suddenly appearing in him. Of course, if they're not, you don't have to continue to go out with him.

The Financial Barrier

Despite the women's liberation movement in the sixties and feminism's rise in popularity, a lot of women—perhaps you included—still want their man to "take care of" them. You'd like for them to pay for dates, buy you nice things, and provide you with a life of luxury. And while this does work for some couples, keep in mind that your partner is not your parent. So, if this is the dynamic in the relationship, make sure that you are offering something in return, like emotional support, home-keeping, or organizing your social life for the two of you so he can focus on work. As long as your relationship is give and take, then it won't feel like this person is your parent.

Not surprisingly, studies done by the Department of Labor asking questions such as "Who makes the decision about how money is spent?" have revealed that wives of blue-collar men (men who earn an hourly wage) have much more power in their relationship than the wives of white-collar men (salaried professionals). In other words, the wealthier the husband, the less powerful the wife. That's because, in relationships, often the partner with the money has the power. So, if you want to get involved with a substantially wealthier man than yourself, that's totally fine, just be sure that you both have equal say in the decisions that will affect both of you. Yes, it is his money, but if he is committed to you and wants your relationship to work and a certain financial decision will affect your relationship, he should care enough to consult you about it.

If you're over thirty years old, *OkCupid.com* found that women who showed some cleavage in their main online photo got many more responses than women who showed an outdoor photo. For those under thirty, the reverse was true! What does this suggest? Perhaps that for women over thirty, men want to see that they've still "got it" and for women in their twenties, men want to see that they actually want to be taken seriously.

SOUL MATE SCENARIOS:
Debbie

After a two-year-long romance, Debbie and John got married. As it turns out, not long after they were betrothed, Debbie became pregnant with twins. The pair agreed that since Debbie felt more comfortable dealing with a corporate environment, and was earning twice John's salary, that she would be the main breadwinner. In return, John chose to take on the majority of the housework and take care of the children. They kept their agreement and though a few of their family and friends questioned their unconventional roles, they knew that they were taking on responsibilities that made each of them happy. Debbie did not consider herself the "boss" in their relationship because she knew what a large service John was doing for the relationship, too. She always consulted him on financial decisions and showed him how grateful she was for the work he did with their kids.

LESSON: Responsibilities can be split in all sorts of ways. It's up to you and your partner—not external sources—to determine what works for your partnership. Many women who believe in the idea of a soul mate think that the perfect man for them will complement them in every way—including how domestic he would like to be. For example, if you always wanted to be a careerwoman, maybe you expect that the perfect man will want to be the domestic one. In this case, if the man you love turns out to not fit that role perfectly, you may think the two of you are not meant to be. But you cannot expect anyone to fit into your lifelong dream perfectly.

Your Homework

If you tend to go for the successful entrepreneurial types, or the high-powered executives, or doctors, or lawyers, give someone who makes less money than you a chance. Or, if you're used to dating guys who make less, try dating someone who makes more. Some of these men may have different characteristics or priorities than you're used to and you might find that you appreciate and like those traits more than those you had been accustomed to.

Loosen Up

Hopefully, by becoming more flexible and by breaking down your dating barriers, you've learned to loosen up your standards regarding physical appearance, financial standing, ethnic and cultural factors, age, and anything else that was closing you off to finding your Mr. Right. In later chapters, we'll explore what factors are necessary for a relationship to progress from attraction to dating to a deeper, more long-term relationship that could result in marriage. But, in the meantime, keep up the good, open-minded work!

THE AFTERMATH EXERCISE

Okay, so now you've run these experiments and gone out with many different types of men—or at least you've started thinking about dating outside your typical type. Get out a piece of paper and write down everything that you've learned from the experience. Feel free to include things like:

- I've learned that men of a different ethnic background can be quite interesting.
- I've learned that I have a lot in common with someone who is younger than me.
- I've learned that I can date blue-collar workers and they are often as interesting as men who are more educated.
- I've learned that handsome men are often just as insecure as less handsome men and that I don't need to feel intimidated by them.
- I've learned that I can enjoy dating a man with children and being with the family.

Soul Mate Summary

By reading through this chapter, hopefully you've learned a few tools and techniques to help you become more flexible when it comes to dating. Just to recap, here's what you should have learned:

- You know what needs you won't compromise on and what wants you'd like to have but don't need to be happy. Certain traits such as honesty, faithfulness, and supportiveness should not be compromised, while other traits such as physical appearance, level of education, wealth, cultural background, and common interests, are desirable but not necessary for a good relationship.

- There is no such thing as "my type." You can be attracted to a variety of men with different characteristics.

- Flexibility is important in finding the personal traits that really matter in a partner for a long-term relationship.

Now it's time to mourn that mythic man so you can get on to meeting your actual Mr. Right!

CHAPTER 5

Grieving
for the
Mythic Man

Right about now you might be still reeling from the new knowledge that your perfect fantasy man—your *one* and *only* soul mate—does not exist. You may have passed up dozens of guys who you now realize had a lot of potential because you were holding out for someone you had never met. Or, you may have passed on them because you were pining after someone from your past—someone you were *certain* you were meant to be with. And now you need to grieve. This concept of grieving when no one has died, you haven't broken up with someone, no one has even moved away may seen a bit drastic, but if you really let the information from the previous chapters sink in, you'll realize that you *have* lost something. You've lost what you thought to be your tried-and-true methods for searching for a mate. And this can leave you feeling a little stranded, just like you do when you actually do lose somebody.

You probably know that grief is an important part of the way humans process intense loss, but you might be thinking, what on earth does grief have to do with me finding Mr. Right? Well, have you ever had a girlfriend who broke up with her long-term boyfriend and never cried about it? It seemed strange, right? That's because if you don't let yourself *feel* the pain, fear, grief, or whatever bad emotions come hand in hand with a "bad" event, then you're really not confronting that event head on. And when you don't deal with something, it can sneak into your subconscious and alter the way you behave and even think. In the case of letting go of the idea of a soul mate, if you don't let yourself feel the fear you might not actually make those changes because emotions, often negative ones at that, are the fuel that motivate you to make change. So grab a tissue box, pop in your favorite movie, do whatever you have to do. You're being instructed to wallow a little. The sooner you get it over with, the sooner you can get back out in the world and apply your new methods of dating to finding a guy who's right for you.

The Five Stages of Grief

In 1969, Psychiatrist Elizabeth Kübler-Ross introduced what became known as "the five stages of grief" within her book *On Death and Dying*. These stages were originally based on her study of people dealing with terminal illnesses, but she later expanded it to apply to other major life changes. In putting to rest your fantasy about someday meeting your soul mate, you can expect to experience each stage of grief. To move on, you must go through each stage before you progress to the next; so don't try to rush this process. Whether you were waiting for a man you never met, or still holding out for that *one* guy you've been trying to get for years, the reality is that that fantasy is *not* reality. Your hopes of getting that guy have to vanish; so he is as real as a lost relative or friend and you have to grieve him as such using these five stages:

1. **Denial:** This can't be happening to me.
2. **Anger:** Why is this happening to me?
3. **Bargaining:** Yes, but what can I do to lessen it?
4. **Depression:** I'm too sad to do anything.
5. **Acceptance:** I'm at peace with what's happening.

In her studies, Kübler-Ross noticed that sometimes people experienced a "roller coaster" effect in which they'd return to stages they'd already passed through and that not everyone processed the stages in the order above or even experienced all of them. However, almost everyone she studied experienced at least two of the stages. Keep this in mind as you take your own feelings into consideration. If you're processing one stage before another or not feeling one of the stages at all, that's okay. You're not "doing it wrong." Everyone's process of grief is extremely personal. The important thing, however, is that when you feel an emotion coming on, don't try to find a distraction. Let it wash over you. Cry for hours if you have to. But don't run away from any of these stages.

Stage One: Denial

Signs that reveal you're in the denial stage:
- You don't really believe that you must give up the fantasy.
- Your behaviors don't change even though they're mired in fantasy.
- You look back on memories you have that are tied to myth.

When you were first told that your fantasy man, the one you've been dreaming about for your whole life, doesn't exist, you were probably a little dumbfounded. That can't be true! Of course he exists!

Shock and disbelief often cushion the blow of loss and can prevent you from feeling overwhelmed. As with the death of a loved one, it's not unusual for you to still feel that this person is there with you even when they're not. If that happens with this mythic man, that's okay. You need to let him go at a pace that works for you. It's okay to still think about this fantasy myth as long as you balance these thoughts with healthy thoughts and actions—and that means actively working towards meeting a suitable partner in real life. After all, while you can't always control what you think—like, you might think, "my soul mate is still out there and he will just fall into my lap, without me doing any work"—you *can* control what you do. So when you have a thought like that, negate it by going out and striking up a conversation with a man who seems interesting. If you actually take an interest in this guy—a guy that you did in fact have to put an effort into finding—you will realize that finding a great partner *is* within your control, and is not controlled by fate.

Be warned, though. Denial is the easiest phase you will experience until you reach acceptance.

SOUL MATE SCENARIOS:
Bernice

Bernice worked at a nursing home and had a crush on a coworker. While Bernice did not really know the man she worked with, he seemed to embody all of the characteristics she wanted in a man. He was handsome, a physician, kind to others, and nearly always appeared to be in a good mood. She knew it was not okay for her to start a relationship with him; first, because the two worked together, and second, because he was married. When Bernice asked me if I thought it would be emotionally okay for her to fantasize about having a relationship with him, I told her that it was okay, just as long as she recognized in her heart that the relationship would not go further than her fantasy. Bernice soon learned to recognize that because this man was "safely unavailable" she could project all her fantasies onto him without having to test them in reality. A similar phenomenon that we can all identify with is a fantasy about your favorite actor. When you don't know the person, even if he does exist in reality, you are still dealing with another variation on the soul mate myth.

LESSON: Anyone can look good if you never experience the reality of actually *being* with them. The trouble with fantasizing about a man is that you begin to compare the men who you actually go on dates with to your fantasy guy, and that comparison is simply unfair! *You* wrote up all the traits of your fantasy guy, so of course he will always seem better than the real guy sitting across from you trying to make a good impression on your date.

So, for your own sake, and for the sake of letting go gradually, it *is* okay to think about the fantasy myth. However, you must also balance that fantasy with healthy thought and action, which means actively working towards meeting a real life partner. You can tell yourself that he is the perfect man for you, and just like that perfect man in your head, if you don't act on the fantasy, he can never disappoint you. As denial and shock wear off, be prepared to enter the next phase in the grieving process.

Stage Two: Anger

Signs that reveal you're in the anger stage:

- You make statements to yourself or others such as "Why me?" or "It always happens to me."
- You make negative statements about the post-myth reality such as "There are no good men out there."
- You envy people who seem to have achieved the myth. In other words, the grass looks greener on the other side.
- Your fuse shortens and you become easily annoyed and irritable with persons and things around you.

Eventually, the shock of denial wears off and you start to feel pain. Sometimes, when pain is great—as it is with grief—it feels like too much to deal with and so we try to find a person or a thing to blame and we direct our pain towards that subject. For example, has your lover ever hurt you emotionally and instead of saying, "What you did hurt me," you lashed out at them in some way? The anger you feel during the grieving process is similar. You focus on how someone else wronged you, rather than on what the emotional implications of that action are for you.

An important thing to keep in mind during this period is that there is a difference between lashing out at someone and sharing with them. Do you know of a friend who, whenever she is upset over a problem with work or her boyfriend, acts like she's aggravated whenever she sees you? Not fair, right? Well, don't be like that. It's fine to share with your friends your fears and pain over your frustrations about finding a man. But do not take out those frustrations on them.

A second thing to keep in mind is that your friends might not even feel bad for you. This doesn't mean that they are insensitive or even that they don't care about you. It simply means that not everyone gets as worked up over certain issues as you do. They may think it's really not that bad that you've suddenly realized that your expectations about love were flawed. They may just not understand how large the implications are for you and how scared you are right now.

But, look on the bright side. At least, in this case, you're grieving for someone who doesn't exist for anyone else either.

SINGLE LADIES

When women sleep with a guy for the first time, it's common for us to wonder what he's thinking afterwards. The good news is that a man is usually thinking some variation of the following:

- That was amazing.
- I hope I did a good job.
- I hope I was big enough for her.
- I'm tired. I'm going to sleep now.
- Wow, I can't wait to do it again.
- I have to do such-and-such tomorrow.

SOUL MATE SCENARIOS:
Katelynn

Katelynn was in her forties and although she had never been married, she had lived with most of her long-term boyfriends. But, she always felt she could do better . . . that her perfect Mr. Right was just around the corner waiting for her. When he didn't show up, Katelynn started to grow angry and, looking back, she realized if she could do it all over again, she would have married one of her previous boyfriends.

Katelynn looked back at a friend from her high school days. Her friend had ended up marrying a guy she met in high school and now each of them had good jobs, had raised several bright children, and, according to Katelynn, appeared to be very happy. What Katelynn didn't realize was that just because her friend seemed happy because she married someone she had met in high school, that didn't mean that Katelynn would have been equally as happy if she had married someone from high school, nor did it mean that the pair was a perfect couple. Perhaps they had arguments that her friend didn't tell her about. It's impossible to know just what goes on in a relationship unless you're actually in it.

LESSON: It's okay to be angry when you're letting go of a fantasy, but don't get angry with yourself for what might have been. You can only make positive, healthy decisions from this point forward. There's no point in regretting the past; it'll only cause you pain.

Stage Three: Bargaining

Signs that reveal you're in the bargaining stage:

- You cross a few demands off your "requirements." Think back to the needs and wants we discussed in the previous chapter.
- You begin to substitute new qualifications that seem more reasonable in place of the older ones.
- You show a friendly interest in men who previously wouldn't have caught your attention.
- You feel less stressed and hard on yourself because you're compromising but staying true to yourself.

And, here's where it starts. "Yes, but. . . . " But, no.

In the denial stage, you're overwhelmed and unable to see what is lying in front of you. In the anger stage, you're basically throwing a tantrum like a child. When you reach the bargaining stage, you start to use a more adult way of maintaining control. In fact, it's here that you might discover that many of the characteristics that you desire in a relationship aren't actually achievable and you start to realize that you won't be able to design your perfect man just as you imagine him to be.

At this time it's not unusual for women to start thinking about ways they could improve themselves in order to possibly still attract that "perfect" guy. You might tell yourself that if you wait a *little* bit longer, he might come around. You'll hang on to any sliver of a chance left that you'll still meet your fantasy man. If this sounds like you, realize that you need to go through this process. If you keep holding on to this idea of a soul mate, you're only prolonging the process of fully letting him go.

SOUL MATE SCENARIOS:
Cara

Cara was thirty-two years old and had never married. She heard her biological clock ticking louder and louder and started to really want to have a child. She looked at her previous list of qualities that she wanted in a man. She began to cross some of them off, such as, he must live within a half hour of me, he must have a full head of hair, and he must be my religion. However, she did not see some of her other demands, such as, he must earn more money than me, he must be within five years of my age, and he must like skiing and tennis, as qualifications that she was willing to discard. She said that she would compromise only because she wanted to get pregnant within the next four or five years. However, she still believed that her extensive list of desirable qualities were actually necessities. She appeared to be willing to try flexibility, but while still holding on to the dream that her myth could materialize into reality.

LESSON: Ladies—when it's time to get real, it's time to get *real*. No one is going to give you a gold medal for letting go of a *few* of your irrational demands. And a relationship isn't likely to manifest that way, either. So long as you are still holding on to the desire for traits that aren't actually necessary for a good relationship—and that are few and far between—you won't be in a good relationship.

Stage Four: Depression

Signs that reveal you're in the depression stage:
- You stop actively pursuing men.
- You lose interest in social activities that were previously rewarding.
- You avoid friends in happy relationships because they make you feel sad.

As luck would have it, just as you reach the most difficult stage, it's about now that the patience or sympathy of those around you has started to decline. Granted, if this were the loss of a spouse, I'd hope your friends would still offer you their shoulder to cry on, but considering you're mourning an idea, you might not have that luxury.

But there's another reason, too. Since you're distraught about not being able to find the perfect partner, listening to you long enough might make your friends start to question their relationships, even if they're in happy ones. And, your single friends might continue to try and reinforce the myth of Mr. Right because they're not ready to go through the same process you're in the middle of.

But, even though you're feeling down in the dumps, try to keep doing those things you did before. That is your one and only responsibility during this phase. Stay active. Being out among people, laughing with your friends, or flirting with a cute guy will remind you that there is life after the soul mate myth. And if you don't force yourself to go out and continue living normally, you could get stuck in this phase for a long time. Possibly forever. You must realize that this too will pass. And, the good news is that as this temporary depression begins to fade, you'll see the dawning of acceptance, the final stage.

SOUL MATE SCENARIOS:
Allison

Allison came to therapy saying that she was depressed because all her efforts to meet "Mr. Right" seem to have led nowhere. One of her complaints was that she no longer enjoyed doing some of the activities, such as skiing and tennis, which she used to enjoy. She said that she didn't enjoy them because she knew that she could not meet her ideal man with these activities. Well, did you ever have to drink medicine when you were feeling sick and did not look forward to drinking it? As a rational adult you realize that you will feel better afterwards and you tolerate the disgust. Sometimes this has to happen when you're depressed. To get out of your funk, take a chance on a new activity that you might enjoy or get back into your old groove with a new attitude. Allison found that by throwing herself into the activities she used to enjoy she felt better about herself even without Mr. Right by her side.

LESSON: If you're struggling to meet someone, now is the time to continue to throw yourself into the activities you love. Why? Because holing up will only make you *more* depressed and if you put out a depressed vibe, you will attract depressed men. Know that you still have the power to enjoy yourself and make yourself happy and, if you're happy, you'll attract the type of guy who's happy too.

Am I Depressed?

Though they might feel similar, there is a difference between the depression associated with a loss and major clinical depression. Here are a few symptoms that will help you tell the difference.

DEPRESSION ASSOCIATED WITH LOSS	MAJOR CLINICAL DEPRESSION
Your feelings are up and down. You feel like you're on a rollercoaster	Your feelings are basically flat.
There is a sudden onset of symptoms.	Your symptoms are chronic and long-term.
Your complaints about loss are specific (in this case, the loss of the mythic man).	There is no specific loss.
Your sadness is associated with certain situations, e.g., family gatherings.	You feel sad in all situations.
Medication does not ease symptoms.	Medication does ease symptoms.
Your depression goes away in six to twelve months.	Your depression is continuous for many years.

CAUTION

If depression persists, or thoughts of suicide occur, it is important to get medical treatment immediately. In some cases, chemical imbalances may need to be reversed before treatment can be helpful. (Read more about the effect of one's chemical processes on relationships in Chapter 2.)

If you feel that you're just grieving your soul mate, try the following:

- Eat a balanced diet full of lots of B vitamins (this vitamin helps in the production of serotonin in the brain).
- Get enough exercise. Exercise raises levels of norepinephrine, dopamine, and serotonin.
- Rest for seven to eight hours every night. During sleep, the brain replenishes its supply of neurotransmitters.
- Get out and be with friends. All social contact stimulates neurotransmitter production. There is positive chemistry between friends and family, as well as lovers.
- Do some things you used to enjoy. This helps even if at first you don't feel like doing anything. Once you get started, the chemicals start flowing and you are reminded of pleasant experiences and feelings once again.

Always remember, if you start to feel depressed and don't think you can handle it on your own, you should set up an appointment with your physician who may refer you to a psychologist.

Stage Five: Acceptance

Signs that reveal you've reached acceptance:
- It no longer hurts to think about the memories associated with the myth.
- You feel an active interest in newer people.
- Your energy level reverts back to what it was previously.
- You look forward to the future.

By the time you reach the acceptance stage, you've already done the hard work. You're able to seek out more positive relationships with a clear head. But, you might be surprised that you may continue to experience the occasional longing for that soul mate you carried with you for so long.

It's important, when this happens, to realize that every human being has fantasies of ideal love and some have been able to attract something awfully close. Now that you're thinking rationally, you're in a much better place to do that. You know what's realistic and you won't toss out every good man you find just because they have this or that forgivable fault. Don't regret your failed relationships. Think of every past experience as a lesson that has made you wiser and stronger. Now, the world is your oyster.

SOUL MATE SCENARIOS:
Eileen

Since she was a teenager, Eileen had a fantasy of a perfect marriage and children. She collected bridal magazines, and had a "hope chest" containing items that she intended to wear at her fancy wedding, store in her future house, and give to her future children. The fantasy, of course, included a groom who had never been married, and would be the father to several children together. At age thirty, realizing that she may remain single forever with only her fantasy man for company, she started to become more flexible. She would now consider men who had already been married, even if they had children. When one man expressed negative attitudes about a big wedding (he was still paying for his first wedding although he was now divorced) Eileen felt disappointed. However she realized that while the big wedding was a one-day experience, the person you lived with afterwards was the important factor. Not soon after this realization, she met Charles. Since he had two teenage boys, and shared joint custody with his ex-wife, the boys lived with him on a bi-weekly basis. Eileen knew immediately that Charles was a package deal. She met the two boys (and later met his ex-wife) and realized that she could get along with the "wife in-law" if necessary, and really liked the two boys. She also enjoyed the activities she engaged in with Charles and his sons. They married; having a medium-sized wedding, with close friends and family members. A year afterward, Eileen became pregnant. While this was not the family she had envisioned as a teenager, she loved her blended family and looked forward to bringing her new baby (a girl) into the mix.

LESSON: Traditional is not necessarily the best. If you believe in the soul mate myth, you may write off any guy who has been married, disturbed by the fact that he has already had a "great love" in his life. But, by now you should know that you can be compatible with many people in your lifetime, as can a man who has been divorced.

Soul Mate Summary

Grief is important for anyone trying to process a loss, whether that loss is of a real person, a significant part of your life, or a fantasy you've held on to for years in the hopes it might one day come true. Within this chapter you've learned:

- How to give yourself permission to grieve that mythic man who has lived in your mind for so long, representing your fantasy or your idealized soul mate.

- That in the process of grieving, you can expect to experience the five stages that victims of any significant loss go through. These stages are denial, anger, bargaining, depression, and acceptance.

- How to recognize the stage that you are in during the grieving process.

- Some coping techniques for each stage of grief that can help to bring you to the next stage in the process.

- That things do get better once you've completed all five stages.

You are now ready to go forward and meet the person who will be your authentic love match.

REBUILDING YOUR IDEAL MAN:

Setting Standards Without Settling

Now that you're open to more types of men and have gone through the grieving process for the mythic man that you couldn't have, you are now ready to pursue a real relationship. The following chapters will provide you with the tools for recognizing authentic love and pursuing the qualities you desire and need in a lifetime partner. You'll also learn the main ingredients of a good relationship, the little things that make a difference, and the dos and don'ts for meeting men and creating and enhancing real relationships. In the end, you will be able to have, not a mythic soul mate, but the real love that you've always dreamed about. It's time to arm you with your handy tool kit for finding love!

CHAPTER 6

Authentic Relationships

The best long-term relationships are based on strong mutual attraction on the physical, mental, and spiritual levels. But, not everyone who stays together for the long term feels these things; sometimes, they stay even though their love is not authentic. How can you tell if the love you feel for your partner is real or if you're trying too hard to find the "perfect" relationship and so you are ignoring the shortcomings of yours? Well, we'll address that within this chapter, but we'll also discuss some of authentic love's biggest building blocks that should be present in every happy, long-term relationship. Together, they'll help you decide whether the guy you're with is Mr. Right or Mr. Wrong (or if not Mr. Wrong, at least just Mr. Right Now).

Nonauthentic Love

Whether you are reading this book because you are having difficulty finding a date; are ambivalent about the man with whom
you are currently involved; or are seeking to improve your long-
term relationship, you're looking to find out exactly what makes
that difference between simple infatuation or lust and an actual
deep connection that won't be shaken easily. This can be less
clear for women than it is for men. Women can make the mistake of thinking they *like* a man and actually want to pursue a
relationship with him just because they feel sexually attracted to
him. Men are often better at carrying on casual sexual relationships. One way that we see this is that men don't usually think
"maybe I could date this woman" just because the two of them
had sex. Women, however, will often fantasize about dating a
guy after sleeping with him and pursue him only to discover that
he isn't all that they had made him out to be in their head. It
may feel like a double standard, but it is a good idea for you to
get to know a guy before sleeping with him so your perspective
on him as a potential partner isn't tainted by the fact that you've
been physically intimate with him. The worst part about having
this happen is that it can be hard to realize something is actually missing from your relationship. Maybe you've always just
had this feeling that *something* is off. If this sounds like you, it's
time to figure out if what's going on is actually normal or if something really is missing. If your relationship contains any of the
following issues, then it's time to start considering channeling
your energies elsewhere.

Jealousy

Jealousy is not a black-or-white issue and even in the best
relationships there will be a *little* bit of jealousy from time to time.
It becomes a problem though when the man (or you) acts on that

jealousy. If he gets angry with you or restricts you from doing certain things due to his jealousy, then he is taking his feelings of insecurity out on you. Rather than making an effort to control his jealousy or face his feelings of insecurity, he makes you feel that you've done something wrong and may even try to control you. However, control has no place in a good relationship. Let me repeat that because it's *very* important: *Control has no place in a good relationship*. If you remain in that relationship his jealousy is likely to just get worse because he interprets your staying with him as an indication that it is okay for him to continue behaving that way. Even worse, you may start to tell yourself that it is okay for him to behave that way because at that point you are so attached that you'd rather stay in an unhealthy relationship than be single. Be alert to signs of jealousy early on so you can assess if this relationship has potential to be a healthy one.

Signs your guy has unhealthy jealousy:

- He texts or calls you often when you're apart because he's suspicious of your behavior.
- He unleashes anger at attractive men who have contact with you.
- He accuses you of cheating when there is no reason for suspicion.
- He's excessively preoccupied with how you look, dress, and speak because he's looking for a slip-up or reason that you might be dressing up that you're not telling him.
- He checks your text messages, e-mail, and Facebook messages.

Drama

Most of our favorite TV couples break up and get back together a dozen times. We tell ourselves it's romantic. We tell ourselves their multiple reunions are a sign of true passion. Well, that's not really the case. That much drama in real life would just be emotionally draining and if you constantly fight and break up, chances are that it is not ever going to stop. So why do some couples in *real* life carry on these soap opera–esque relationships? Because while they're attracted to each other, they have key incompatibilities that they're either not willing or not able to work through. For example, one person may love to spend most of their free time with their family; while the other may prefer to be alone with their partner. One may be very religious, while the other has barely any religious or spiritual interest. One person may place a high value on work and financial success, while the other may be more motivated towards pleasurable activities, preferring to have more time than money. Just remember: Passion is great in a relationship. Drama is not.

Signs your relationship is too dramatic:

- You speak to one another in loud voices with intense gestures.
- Your mood swings from elation to depression to anger and love (i.e., the rollercoaster effect).
- You think about the other person so much that other areas of your life (work, home, friendships, etc.) become affected.
- It is hard to separate from each other even for a short time.
- Others are uncomfortable around you and your partner because there is almost always a storm brewing between the two of you.

Outside Pressures

Usually, when a couple is in love, their friends and families are supportive, but this isn't always the case. Sometimes your family or friends might not be actually looking at the relationship but judging it with their own biases. They might not approve of the religion, the race, or the culture of the person you're dating. They might not approve of how much they make. They might not approve of what your partner looks like if his style is different from theirs. If you feel that these are the real reasons they don't approve of your beau, then by all means, don't worry about their opinion. It's not your fault they're being close-minded.

But, most times, the people close to you just want you to be happy. And, if they see the way you light up when you talk about the person you're with and they see that he treats you with kindness and respect, they'll be happy for you and supportive of the relationship. But, if they're not being supportive, ask yourself, are they holding up a mirror for you to show you things you've been unable to see? They may be trying to reveal to you that you don't seem very happy in the partnership and that maybe there is someone else out there that will be a better match. Think about it: you have probably had friends who were in terrible relationships and you were able to see that very clearly, while they remained oblivious to the fact that anything was wrong. It can happen to anyone, even to you.

Abuse

Abuse is *never* okay and it's one very clear sign that you are not in a loving, happy relationship. But, abuse can take multiple forms. Physical abuse in the form of violence is the most obvious, and if you're in a physically abusive relationship, you need to get out immediately. But even if your partner has never hit you or abused you physically doesn't mean that the relationship isn't abusive. Other signs of abuse include:

- Your partner criticizes, insults, or puts you down.
- Your partner asks you to do things that they know make you uncomfortable.
- Your partner provokes your jealousy through flirting, etc. with others when you are around.
- Your partner insults or criticizes you to your friends or family in an attempt to isolate you from your other support systems.
- Your partner engages in excessive teasing, taunting, and negative behaviors (even if your partner later states that this behavior was only a joke).

Now, there is a clear line between abuse and playful physical interactions. Pillow fights, tickle wars, wrestling each other in bed, and other such ways of physically interacting with your partner are okay. They bring back a childlike sense of play into the relationship, and that's good. Even playfully teasing each other is a good thing, as long as it's done in a loving way.

However, it can be hard to exactly put your finger on *how* the person is being abusive or not so just trust your heart. If you have to start rationalizing your partner's actions, if you already know that something is going on that isn't right, or if you realize that your partner is trying to control you, it's time you hightailed it out of there. Fast.

Sacrifice

There's a difference between sacrifice and compromise. Within every relationship—be it friendly, familial, or romantic—there will be compromise. You are not going to get your way all of the time. If you did, you'd have a very unhappy—and probably spineless—partner. So, you two need to meet in the middle.

Let's take football and shopping as an example. It's Sunday and you want your partner to go shopping with you. He'd rather watch football, but, he agrees to do what you want to do. The next Sunday, you want to go out to dinner but he wants to watch football, especially since he didn't get to watch the game last weekend. Instead of insisting he goes out to dinner with you, you compromise and decide to order in or make dinner at home and then sit down and watch the game with him. Is it what you really want to be doing? No, but it will elicit good feelings between you and your partner. Equal compromise is good. But when only one person compromises, things can turn ugly—and that's when the compromise becomes more of a sacrifice. True sacrifice means giving up something that's good for you only to satisfy someone else. And a partner who cares about you would never request that you do that. Some examples of unacceptable sacrifice include:

- You lend money that you cannot afford to your partner.
- You engage in sex acts that make you uncomfortable.
- You are okay with allowing infidelity or lack of commitment if it satisfies your partner.
- You tolerate any type of abuse: physical, emotional, or verbal.
- You make any significant life change such as moving, giving up your career, or having a child only to please your spouse.

Pressure

When someone loves you, they will not pressure you into doing something that is not good for you. They might try to get you to do something you're uncomfortable with—say, try new foods or go zip lining or fly if you're afraid of flying—but they will only do these things if they know it's in your best interest.

However, if your partner is trying to pressure you into something that goes against your deep moral values (like trying to get you to eat meat if you're a vegetarian) or causes you extreme discomfort (like threatening to leave you if you don't go with them to a swingers party), then that's a problem because they're trying to control you and they are able to enjoy themselves even when you are clearly unhappy. And, as we've discussed, control does not belong in an authentic relationship.

The ultimate decision rests with you. If you feel that something is wrong, it usually is. That does not mean that your partner is deliberately making you uncomfortable; but it does mean that the two of you have a few things to discuss. If it turns out that you cannot resolve important differences, such as what constitutes playfulness and what constitutes excessive teasing and controlling, then perhaps your personalities are incompatible. That is why, although you don't need to see eye to eye on everything, you do need to be comfortable with one another's values, preferences, sense of humor, and views regarding respect for one another. For a couple to remain in a serious relationship, they must be on the same page regarding these matters. And don't be afraid to talk to your partner about what's going on. You may tell yourself, "If this person was my soul mate, I would never feel like anything was wrong" and just drop the relationship, but there isn't a person out there with whom you will *never* experience *any* tension. And if you simply address something you are unhappy about, your partner may be able to make adjustments that eliminate that tension. But this can't happen if you are not honest and upfront about being unhappy with a certain dynamic.

Many women, whether they're single or not, ask whether they should fake an orgasm. The answer is definitely not. If you fake it, you're essentially telling him that what he did in bed was successful and he'll keep doing that move, angle, etc. so that you come every time. Instead, try to help him by showing him what works for you. Don't tell him he's doing it wrong, but guide him so he can learn how to do it right. Remember, honesty is always important in an authentic relationship.

Evidence of Authentic Love

Now that you know what you don't want to look for in a relationship, it's time to talk about what you *do* want: authentic love, a love that has stood the test of time and challenges. Authentic love is tied to reality, not fantasy. If you buy into the soul mate myth, you may want an immediate connection and understanding with someone, but authentic love takes time to develop; it sees flaws and doesn't seek perfection. It does not focus on superficialities, such as physical appearance or financial status. Rather, it is based upon shared values and goals, mutual respect, and caring for one another. If you are experiencing authentic love, you place the same value upon your partner's needs as you do upon your own. In authentic relationships, there is a deep friendship and a sexual attraction. But there are other factors as well.

Mutual Self-Disclosure

As you get to know your partner, you'll discover things about them that will give you the indication that you'll want to stick around or that you'll want to bolt out the door. While some of these things may be readily apparent or revealed within your first few conversations, you might not learn about others until later down the line. For instance, say your partner has a lot of debt they're working to pay off. That's not something you'll probably find out about on the first date, or the second, or maybe the third.

While the nature of this information is important, so is the way they reveal it to you. Does he offer up the information freely or do you have to stumble upon some evidence? Does he become defensive about it, or does he speak to you about it in a way that lets you know that he is comfortable showing his flaws to you? Everyone has flaws and may have even made large mistakes like getting into debt or having married the wrong person and gotten a divorce. This doesn't make them a bad person or a bad partner. It only becomes a problem when your partner tries to hide these flaws or mistakes or becomes noticeably unhappy when they are brought up. This indicates unresolved issues and insecurities that could affect your relationship in the long run.

Balance

There are four areas that are important to keep in balance within a relationship:

- Power
- Responsibility
- Vulnerability
- Support

In authentic relationships, there shouldn't be power struggles, and one person shouldn't feel significantly more vulnerable or emotionally invested than the other. That said, sometimes you might find that your partner goes through a low period during which he can't give you as much support as usual—and he may even need more support from you than usual. If the relationship has proven to be balanced in the previously mentioned ways most of the time, then it's important for you to try and support him just as he should support you if you hit a rough patch. But neither you nor your partner should be expected to carry the other forever and you should expect him to do the work necessary to try and get back on his own feet.

Finally, when it comes to responsibility, balance does not necessarily mean splitting everything exactly equally. For instance, if one person makes more money, that person might pay for more dinners out while the other person makes an effort to cook at home more often or take on more responsibility in another area. Keep in mind that responsibility isn't about *how* much two people in a relationship give one another, but rather that they are both giving as much as they are capable of. In the end, you're going to enjoy the fact that your partner thought of what he had to offer you and gave that to you even more than a beautiful gift or a delicious meal.

Communication

For a couple to succeed in an authentic committed relationship, good communication is a must. Without communication, you will likely end up accepting dynamics in your relationship that you are unhappy with because you couldn't communicate your dissatisfaction to your partner. But communication isn't a one-way street. Your partner should make you feel comfortable and safe communicating with him as well. And once he does this, it's up to you to let him know if you are unhappy.

A very common mistake that both men and women in every type of relationship make is not saying when something upsets them the first time, and then finally exploding when it happens too many times. This is unfair to the other person because if you had just told him that something upset you the first time it happened, he would have had the chance to remedy it and avoid having you explode. Good communication is the key to a happy, healthy future with anyone. Without it, even the sturdiest-seeming relationship will eventually crumble. The soul mate myth really plays on our laziness to communicate. Most women who believe in the soul mate myth believe that they don't have to convey their feelings or thoughts to their partner—that he will just *know* what they're thinking. These women will often leave a man the moment there is a misunderstanding, because that indicates to her that the man is not her soul mate. Does that sound reasonable to you? The following quiz will give you an idea of where you and your partner stand when it comes to communicating on difficult issues.

COMMUNICATION QUIZ

Simply mark true or false for the following statements. Then, have your partner take the test and compare your answers. Discuss your findings.

1. I often can't seem to find the right words to express what I want to say.　True　False

2. I worry that exposing myself to my partner will result in rejection.　True　False

3. I often don't talk because I am afraid my opinion is wrong.　True　False

4. Speaking openly makes things worse.　True　False

5. I talk too much and don't give my partner a chance to speak.　True　False

6. I don't look forward to talking to my partner.　True　False

7. Once I get started in an argument, I have trouble stopping.　True　False

8. My speech is often defensive.　True　False

9. I frequently bring up my partner's past infractions.　True　False

10. My actions often don't match what I say.　True　False

11. I often don't really listen.　True　False

12. I try to repay anger with anger or insult with insult.　True　False

13. I tease my partner until he gets angry.　True　False

14. I don't like listening when my partner brings up a problem.　True　False

15. I think it's important to lay out all the complaints I have about him to my partner.　True　False

16. I state my complaints in a very heated manner.　True　False

17. I tend to say "you always" or "you never" when discussing my complaints with my partner.　True　False

18. I rarely state my complaints to keep from hurting my
    partner.   True   False

19. I have a hard time seeing things from my partner's point of
    view.   True   False

20. I don't like to argue because I feel arguing means we don't have a good
    relationship.   True   False

21. In an argument, I would rather be right than compromise.   True   False

22. I don't like to discuss negative feelings because it only makes us feel
    worse.   True   False

23. I don't feel I should have to bring up what's bothering me because my
    partner should already know.   True   False

Scoring

Give yourself one point for every false and give yourself zero points for
every true.

Interpretation

If your point score is between 17 and 24, you have good communication
skills. If your point score is between 9 and 17, you have average communication
skills. If your point score is an 8 or lower, your communication skills need some
work before you're ready for an authentic romantic relationship. But, in addition to knowing how good of a communicator you are, you also want to know if
you're an active or a passive communicator.

Passive Communicator

If you answered 1–4, 21, or 23 true you might be a passive communicator.
This means that you don't often express negative opinions because you're afraid
of rejection. You might have been raised in a family where you were taught to
be very polite or you were often rebuked or punished in some way for saying or
doing the wrong thing. To communicate effectively within an authentic relationship, you need to learn to express yourself respectfully, but assertively.

Aggressive Communicator

If you answered 9, 10, 13, 16–19, or 22 true, you might be an aggressive communicator. This means you tend to become defensive and make accusatory statements such as "You are X, Y, or Z" instead of trying to see things from your partner's perspective or realizing what part you are playing in the conflict.

If this is a habit of yours, sometimes it's better to wait to discuss something until you are ready to discuss the topic in a calm, collected, adult way so that you do not hurt your partner. Remember, your partner is not your enemy. Even though the two of you might be disagreeing on a matter, you can still see them as an ally and respect their opinion even if you don't agree with it. Doing so will lead to a deeper understanding between you both and a more loving, authentic relationship.

Healthy Conflict Resolution

Healthy conflict resolution is an essential component of authentic love. Often women stay stuck in the soul mate myth because they do not wish to ever experience conflict with their partner. This goes back to some of the fears that we discussed in Chapter 3, fear of rejection, fear of abandonment, fear of engulfment, and fear of vulnerability. Often these fears originated in one's family of origin. You may have seen excessive conflict that was unsuccessfully resolved, thereby generating a hostile family environment. Or your past relationships may have been negative, abusive, or simply ended once conflict arose. If that has been a pattern in your past, you may hope to find someone who is exactly like you (your soul mate) so that you will never have to experience the trauma of conflict. Since, as you learned in the preceding chapters, such a soul mate does not exist, it is necessary to learn healthy methods of conflict resolution. Every couple fights. It's how you fight that matters. That means no name-calling, dish-throwing, or temper tantrums. Follow this fair-fighting guide and you and your mate will both emerge victorious.

Establish Goals

Men think in a very bottom-line, get-to-the-point sort of way. After you've stated what's wrong, tell him what you'd ideally like to see accomplished and, if it's applicable, ask him what his goals are regarding the topic on the table. You can say something as simple and direct as "I wish you would XYZ more. Are you willing to do that or can you do that?"

Be Direct

State the facts clearly; then state your feelings. Remember to use "I" statements, such as "I feel bad when you do that."

Stay away from accusatory "you" statements like, "You made me feel bad." Also refrain from hiding "you" statements in "I" statements, such as "I feel that you wanted to hurt me." You don't know why your partner did what they did because you don't live inside their head. You only know how it made you feel. So, if it sounds accusatory, don't say it. The point is not to make your partner feel bad, it's to make yourself feel better. And the only information your partner really needs is how you are feeling. If he cares about you, he will think of a way to make you feel better or accept your suggestions of how he can do that.

Practice Active Listening

It's important for your partner to feel like they are being heard. Listen attentively while your partner is talking, and then quickly summarize their point by saying something akin to, "So what you're saying is. . . . " Only respond after you assure your partner that you're both on the same page.

SINGLE LADIES

According to OkCupid.com, six months is statistically the time when both men and women start to wonder if they should say those special three words to their partner. If you want to encourage him to say it first, continue to do things that show him you love him and see how he responds: make him his favorite meal. Get him something at the store—just because. Eventually, if he still hasn't said it after more time has passed and you're not sure where he stands, you can say it first to test the waters.

Get Some Perspective

While it's easy to see things from only your point of view, step into your partner's shoes for a moment and try to see things from his perspective. Remember, just because his opinion differs from yours doesn't mean it's wrong. Think about his upbringing. Think about the current circumstances in his life—his stresses at work or with his family, certain pressures he might be under— to avoid overreacting and just thinking your partner is totally unreasonable or unfair.

Talk Less

Don't just go on and on about the issue. It's easy to want immediate confirmation that your partner understands what you're thinking and feeling, so you end up repeating yourself. But you won't really know that he understood the problem until you see him implementing a solution. So just state the issue once and then move on to discussing solutions.

Learn to Compromise

Relationships are about compromise. Most times, some middle ground can be found, even if the solution isn't ideal. Remember, the point isn't to "win" and get your way, because you will only end up being unhappy when you can feel how unhappy your partner is. Try to find a compromise you can both agree on—because if you don't both agree on it, then you really haven't solved anything.

CONFLICT RESOLUTION TEST

Are you and your partner good at conflict resolution? Take the following quiz and see how you stack up and where your problem areas lie so you can address them.

1. If I am upset about something, I have to let my partner know immediately.   True   False

2. I try to resolve all conflicts before they grow too big.   True   False

3. I have to raise my voice to get my partner to listen to me.   True   False

4. When I am angry about something, I can't enjoy anything.   True   False

5. Many times I don't voice that I'm upset because I want to avoid confrontations.   True   False

6. I show contempt and anger towards my partner when he doesn't agree with me.   True   False

7. I point out all the ways that he was at fault when we have an argument. True   False

8. I can't help it if I'm right more often. I have to let that be known. True   False

9. Sometimes when I am upset, I am so emotional I have difficulty communicating.   True   False

10. When other people are around, I often criticize my partner.   True   False

11. After an argument, I sometimes am ashamed and feel bad about some of the things I said.   True   False

Scoring and Interpretation

Give yourself one point for every false answer. If you scored between 8 and 10, you are great at resolving conflicts. If you scored 5 to 7, you have some work to do on maintaining your cool and fighting fair with your partner. When you find yourself getting too emotional, take a few moments off and then return to the discussion when you are calmer. If you scored 0 to 4, you may have difficulty resolving conflicts in a healthy way. Reread the section on conflict and consider going to couples, counseling to learn some healthy ways to disagree.

The Long Haul

Eventually, if you're in a happy, authentic relationship, there comes a time when you will decide if this person will be your partner for the rest of your life. After all, a life partner isn't just someone with whom you enjoy vacations and dates. Rather he's someone who will help you through the tiresome, painful, and even ugly sides of life, and he's the person with whom you want most to celebrate the exciting parts. The good news is that there are some questions that you can ask yourself and your partner that will help show you whether or not he will make a good life partner. To avoid seeming neurotic, you can just ask yourself many of these questions silently instead of handing him a typed up questionnaire. But there will be a few for which you won't know the answer without asking him. The following questionnaire will also give you some ideas about how you feel overall about your current partner. Yes, he irritates you sometimes. But you may realize that, while he isn't perfect, his negative traits are not that hard to deal with. You might also realize that even though he doesn't meet *many* (or even any) of the traits your mythical soul mate does, you still love him. After you've thought about each and every one of his traits that can drive you up the wall, you might realize that the overriding feeling for him is still love.

For those that questions that are of particular importance to you, make sure to listen closely to what your partner is saying. His body language, tone, and facial expressions along with his words will tell you how deeply he feels about a topic and will give you an indication if there is room for compromise or change. Just like at the beginning of the relationship when you paid close attention to any traits of his that might cause later pain, you now have to pay just as close attention to a whole other slew of traits—those that relate to the long haul. And just like in the beginning, you want to know now so as to avoid future strife. So don't overlook a disagreement on a core issue.

Family History

- What was your partner's relationship with his mother?

  _____

- What was your partner's relationship with his father?

  _____

- What was your partner's relationship with his brothers?

  _____

- What was your partner's relationship with his sisters?

  _____

- What was your partner's relationship with his grandparents?

  _____

- What did your partner like most about his family?

  _____

- What did your partner like least about his family?

  _____

- What was your partner's parents' relationship with one another?

  _____

Cultural Background

- What ethnic background is your partner's father?

  _____

- What ethnic background is you partner's mother?

  _____

- What about your partner's grandparents' ethnic background? Were they born in this country or another country?

  _____

- Was your partner born in this country? If not, what was their country of origin?

  _____

- What language was your partner's primary language?

  _____

- How strongly was your partner educated about his ethnic background?

  _____

- How does your partner feel about you and persons of your ethnic background?

  _____

Religion and Spirituality

- What is your partner's religion?

  _____

- Does he consider himself to be a serious follower of his religion?

  _____

- What were your partner's parents' attitudes towards religion?

  _____

- What is your partner's attitude towards spirituality?

  _____

- How does your partner feel about your religious views?

  _____

- Are you and your partner similar or different as far as your religious views are concerned? If different, how will you resolve these differences?

  _____

Health Issues

- Does your partner or any of his family members have a history of genetic diseases that he is aware of?

  _____

- Does your partner have any chronic illnesses? Physical? Mental?

  _____

- Is there a history of alcohol or drug abuse in your partner's family? If so, is that person in recovery?

  _____

- Does your partner have a history of drug or alcohol abuse? (Caution: Denial is a major factor here. You may have to rely upon your own sense of what constitutes a serious drug or alcohol problem).

  _____

- What is your partner's attitude towards smoking, drinking, drug use? Is it similar to your attitude? If there are differences, how will you resolve these differences?

  _____

- Does your partner have any sexually transmitted diseases?

  _____

- Has your partner ever had any sexually transmitted disease?

  _____

Relationship History

- Can your partner describe his most passionately intense relationship?

  _____

- What are your partner's ideas on commitment and long-term relationships?

  _____

- What are your partner's ideas about children? Does he want any? How many?

  _____

- What are your partner's ideas about living together, getting married, or living apart?

  _____

- What is your partner's history with the above? Has he ever been married? Has he ever lived with anybody?

  _____

- How has your partner handled previous breakups?

  _____

- What does your partner like most in women?

  _____

- What does your partner like least in women?

  _____

- What is your partner's belief in monogamy? Does it mesh with yours?

  _____

Financial History

- What is your partner's family's attitude towards money?

  _____

- Is your partner a spender or a saver?

  _____

- How does he feel about your spending habits?

  _____

- Can you and your partner compromise on what is important financially?

  _____

- Was your partner raised wealthy, middle class, or poor?

  _____

- Was your own financial history growing up wealthy, middle class, or poor?

  _____

- How do you feel about saving?

  _____

- How do you feel about spending?

  _____

- Do you think financial resources should be pooled in a couple's relationship or kept separate?

  _____

- Does your partner have any major debt?

  _____

- Do you have any major debt?

  _____

- How does your partner feel about that?

  _____

Legal History

- Is your partner involved in any lawsuits or legal actions?

  _____

- Has your partner ever been arrested?

  _____

- Has your partner ever been in jail?

  _____

- If your partner has a legal history, what were the specific incidents that created the problem?

  _____

- Do you have any history of involvement with the law?

  _____

- How does your partner feel about this?

  _____

Critical Incidents

- Was your partner ever a victim of physical abuse?

  _____

- Was your partner ever the perpetrator of physical abuse?

  _____

- Was your partner ever the victim of sexual abuse?

  _____

- Was your partner ever the perpetrator of sexual abuse?

  _____

- What are your answers to the above questions? Were you ever a victim of sexual or physical abuse?

  _____

- Can you share this with your partner?

  _____

- How does he feel about this?

  _____

- How does it affect you in current relationships?

  _____

- Does your partner have a history of serious mental illness? If so, what type? What kind of treatment is he receiving? Is it working?

  _____

- Do you have a history of serious mental illness? If so, what kind of treatment are you receiving? Is it working?

  _____

A lot of these questions are very personal, but most issues that come up in relationships stem back to these issues. Many couples end up struggling with these issues because they didn't want to or were not ready to share personal details about their lives. And there isn't something wrong with you if you answered yes to the more unpleasant questions above. The problem arises if you have not dealt with these issues. If you, for example, haven't seen a therapist to deal with issues of abuse or if you haven't seen a financial counselor to deal with debt, then these issues will sneak up and affect your relationship in unexpected ways. Authentic love only occurs when you can be upfront with your partner about pretty much everything. That way he can better understand why you behave certain ways and vice versa. He can even help you solve any problems that you may be struggling with. If you already know the honest answer to the above questions and are *comfortable* with the answers, knowing they will not negatively affect your relationship, then you could be on your way to a lifetime partnership with this person.

IS HE AT PEACE?

Just because a man tells you about his problems, does not mean he is at peace with them. Is he calm when he brings them up? Is he able to joke about them? On the flip side does he show excessive anger or judgment towards others who struggle with the same issue? Or stiffen up when the issue is mentioned? There is a difference between being open yet *defensive* and being open and at peace. Pay attention to see which one he is.

Soul Mate Summary

After reading this chapter hopefully you know what an authentic relationship looks like so you can either find one or recognize whether or not the one you are in is authentic. If you are unsure if the relationship you are in is authentic or are having trouble finding one, keep the following points in mind:

- In an authentic relationship, there are some core conditions that must be fulfilled. These include respect, healthy conflict resolution, open communication, and honesty with one another. While you may not be soul mates, you need to see eye-to-eye on important issues regarding values and long-term goals.

- There are positive ways to disagree with your partner. These include open communication, "I statements," leading to assertive rather than aggressive communication, acknowledgment and respect for one another's points of view, and a genuine effort to address one another's needs.

- Types of communication to avoid in an argument include insults, put-downs, accusations, or "you statements," implying that your partner is to blame for your negative feelings. You should also avoid thinking about unrelated issues, opinions of friends or family, and reminders of past incidents.

- There are certain facts that you need to know about one another if you are considering becoming life partners. These include attitudes regarding family, children, values, history, and any significant physical and mental health issues.

As we move forward, the next two chapters will provide more suggestions for enhancing your relationship and ensuring its long-term potential.

CHAPTER 7

The Main
Ingredients

You've learned a lot about relationships by now. You've con-
quered fears, you've addressed your needs and desires, and
you've just learned what's required for a relationship to be
authentic—and what definitely shouldn't be in the mix. Now,
it's time for you to start looking at the relationship as a whole.
Yes, it's important to keep your own identity. It's important to
keep doing the things that make you *you,* relationship or not.
But, there comes a time in every relationship when you should
feel comfortable and even *want* to put the relationship before
other components of your life. Now, you don't need to be that
woman who constantly cancels plans on her friends in favor of
being with her man, but you don't want to put your relationship
after everything else either. When you are truly close and connected to a man, you need to bump him up on your priorities
list. Because at some point he is no longer just your boyfriend
—he is your partner. And in order for a partnership to work,
sometimes each individual in it has to compromise for the good

of the partnership. That could mean giving up a girl's night out here or there, but you know your partner will support you when you ask him to cancel something too.

But, what else does your relationship need to have to work long term? Because even once you've met a guy who seems perfect in every way as an individual, in order for the relationship to work, there are some expectations that should be filled in terms of how the two of you interact. Here you'll learn about some realistic expectations that you should have for love, your relationship, and for the man who will be your lifelong—or at least long-term—partner.

Compatibility

You learned about the importance of chemical compatibility in Chapter 1 and understand that this factor influences the attraction phase in regards to who you find appealing; as well as the later phases of romance and attachment. This type of compatibility ensures that you partner with the person with whom you are biologically likely to produce healthy offspring. We've also discussed compatibility in terms of views on important matters like religion, family, fidelity, culture, and other external factors that can affect a relationship, but here we are going to discuss a different type of compatibility that focuses more on personality and your emotional affinity with your partner.

Here, compatibility means that your similarities work well together and your differences are complementary as opposed to antagonistic. In practical terms, you work well as a team. You like one another, you feel comfortable with one another, you have the flexibility to adjust to each other's needs, you don't experience that many conflicts, and you both have a sense of being "in sync."

Here are some signals that you and your partner might be compatible:

- You can't help but smile every time you see him and he is usually smiling back.
- You feel comfortable and secure in the relationship and you trust your partner not to hurt you.
- There are good times and bad times, yet you still remain together and feel close to one another.
- You do kind and thoughtful things for him and he does the same. Doing these things for one another makes you both happy.
- You enhance one another. Each one sees the other person as someone who "brings out the best in them."
- Sex is an important part of the relationship, but you feel happy even if sex is not involved for short periods of time.

Compatibility Questions

Here are some important questions to consider when trying to figure out if you and your mate are compatible:

1. Do you and your partner enjoy being in each other's company? This is important. You may not share every single interest, but you must find each other's company enjoyable enough so that, even when you're not enjoying the activity you're doing, having your partner there makes it bearable.

2. Do you and your partner respect each other's individuality? This means allowing your partner to do things alone that make him happy, as long as it doesn't hurt the relationship. Healthy people can move towards one another but they also have appropriate boundaries. You are more than half of a couple. You are each individuals who also come together.

3. Does your partner fuel your self-esteem and make you feel competent to take on other parts of your life? Do you feel comfortable sharing your downfalls with your partner and do you feel better after having spoken to him? You should both provide positive support systems to one another and also work on your own to make yourselves happy and strong. If you're in a relationship where one person is constantly trying to lift the other one out of a self-defeated and even depressed place, this is not a healthy relationship. The person who is not strong as an individual will only drain the other one of energy. Instead you want a relationship based on mutual positivity.

These factors are the things that make everyday living a pleasure for both you and your partner. When you are right for one another, there is a sense that you complete each other, not in a fantasy way, but in a more mature fashion.

A GOOD MATCH? TEST

If you're currently in a relationship with a guy and you're trying to figure out if he's a good match, here's a quick test to see if he's worth keeping around for the long haul.

1. I feel safe and secure in his presence.   True   False

2. I trust him completely.   True   False

3. We share intimate details about ourselves with each other.   True   False

4. My friends and family like him and think we are a good match.
   True   False

5. I am comfortable in his presence for long periods of time.   True   False

6. When I feel down, he's the person I go to first.   True   False

7. He respects my opinions and feelings.   True   False

8. I could picture spending the rest of my life with him.   True   False

9. I have not seriously considered being with another man since I met him.   True   False

10. He has some negative habits but I can live with all of them.   True   False

Scoring and Interpretation

For each true answer, give yourself one point. If you scored between 8 and 10, it looks like this guy could very well be your Mr. Right. If you scored between 5 and 7, the two of you might face some bumps in your journey together, but they could probably be worked out if you both want to share your future together. If you scored between 0 and 4, there might be too many differences for you two to be happy with each other in the long run.

No matter how madly in love you may be, everyone needs space sometimes. And that's a good thing! You want a man who has an identity of his own and doesn't just cling to you every second. So if your partner wants a night to go out with his friends or even just have a quiet night alone, let him have it. He'll be even happier to see you next time! But pay attention to why he is asking for space. If he has a fear of engulfment, that can be an issue. You don't want to be with a man who "needs space" every hour, or even every day, really! If you sense your partner has a fear of engulfment, address it. Find out now if it's something he wants to work through so you can decide if this relationship is one that you want to stay in.

Intelligence

This might be hard to swallow, but it's *okay* for one person to be intellectually superior in a relationship. After all, there are many different types of intelligence. If your partner is a tech geek and you can barely work a keyboard, fine! You're most likely knowledgeable about things he knows nothing about. Even if you both have your own intellectual merits, in many relationships one person somehow still arises as the apparently more intelligent one. Don't let that disparity get to you. As long as you still enjoy talking to one another, learning, and teaching one another, your intelligence difference won't cause a problem. After all, there's a reason the whole teacher-student concept is sexy.

Just be sure that your partner finds your knowledge interesting and vice versa. If he is constantly rambling on about a subject that you think is insignificant, then you may have a problem. But if you love to talk politics and he was a political science major in college, this could make for a lot of engaging conversations that will leave the two of you feeling closer.

Of course there will be *some* topics you love to discuss that he has no interest in and vice versa and this doesn't always mean you aren't a good match. Ideally, your partner will be able to engage you in interesting conversations when you bring up a topic that is dear to your heart. But, when it comes to the less important areas or issues, if your partner isn't as interested, find a group or a friend who can satisfy your desire to discuss those ideas. Do you dump every guy who loves to talk sports? No. He has his guy friends to talk to about that and you have certain things you only discuss with your girlfriends. This doesn't have to sabotage the relationship.

SELF-EXPANSION

In a relationship what's important is not just the ways you get along, but the ways you teach each other as well. In 2010, Dr. Arthur Aron of the Interpersonal Relationships Laboratory and Dr. Gary Lewandowski, Jr., of Monmouth University examined a phenomenon between couples known as self-expansion, the belief that your partner should be a resource that enhances your self-growth. The researchers found that couples who saw their partner as a resource to enhance their own growth and self-esteem were happier in their marriages than those who did not. So, teach your partner what you know and never stop learning!

Morals and Values

Likely, you're not even friends with people whose morals and values are much different than yours. If you had a friend who thought lying was okay and you thought it was morally reprehensible except in dire circumstances, then the pair of you might not be friends for very long. The same goes for relationships. When it comes to what is right and what is wrong, it's important for you and your man to see eye-to-eye—especially on the following topics:

- Religious views
- Attitude towards children
- Attitude towards parents
- Cultural respect
- Political views
- Attitude towards money
- Honesty and trust
- Attitude towards sex
- Meaning of commitment and marriage
- Attitude towards drug and alcohol use
- Attitude towards in-laws
- Educational values
- Work-related ethics
- Attitude regarding illness or long-term care
- Attitude about conflict resolutions

If you and your partner don't see eye-to-eye on these important moral areas you can bet that you're going to get into some pretty nasty arguments at a later date. And, worse, it'll be very difficult to find your way out of them!

Keep the Following in Mind

In addition to the similarities we just discussed it's also important for you to consider the following when making a decision about who will eventually be your lifelong partner:

1. Do you and your partner have similar values and long-term goals? For example, in five years, does one of you hope to have a modest home in a suburban area where you can raise children while the other hopes for the two of you to be jet-setting? Do you wish for the same experiences out of your relationship? This is essential beyond the romantic stage if you will continue in a long-term relationship.

2. How well have the two of you weathered hardship or the test of time? Many happy couples are absolutely shocked to see how one another behave in difficult situations. Determine whether or not he will be helpful or just more stressful in difficult situations, which, by the way, there will be plenty of in life.

3. Does your relationship have the capacity for forgiveness? Are you able to get past difficult statements, harsh words, and outside difficulties without continuous anger and blame? You see some couples who remind one another constantly, "Well, you did X, Y, Z!" and you can't help but wonder, if they're obviously still so hurt by a past event, why are they still together?

These factors are important indicators of whether or not your relationship will be successful, once you have to incorporate your partner into other parts of your life—like your work and your family—if the two of you are going to stay together. If you are in it for the long haul (the attachment phase), then your answers to the above questions should be positive, but this doesn't mean that you and your partner have to be similar in all things. In fact, there are times when differences between partners actually work to enhance the relationship.

Complementary Differences

Opposites attract? Well, sort of. They can also just end up repelling one another. It just depends on *which* traits you differ on. If the two of you have completely different morals and especially different views for the relationship, then no matter how exciting it was to have some disagreements in the beginning, you're just going to end up being in constant disagreement later.

But *personality* traits are a different story. If you love to be the center of attention but in fact don't trust or are even annoyed by men who are the center of attention, you will probably get along most with a quieter type who is happy to take the back seat as you do all the entertaining when you're out with friends. If you are a very contemplative type who is slow to take action, you may match well with a more adventurous type who will prompt you to try new things. You can see there is a big difference between being opposite and being complementary.

ANTAGONISTIC DIFFERENCES

Whereas there are some differences that bring a couple closer together, antagonistic differences don't work out so well. However, it's difficult to tell if differences will be complementary or antagonistic. That simply differs from couple to couple. Each couple has a unique chemistry; however, some likely antagonistic differences include:

- One person wants to have many children; the other person hates kids.

- One person loves to spend money; the other person is extremely frugal and resents the big spender.
- One person loves social activities and wants friends and family surrounding the couple constantly; the other person hates having a lot of people around and wants to stay alone with their partner.

In the end, whether a difference hurts or helps the relationship depends upon how both partners handle and interpret the particular difference.

SOUL MATE SCENARIOS:
John and Alice

John and Alice have been happily married for fifteen years and friends often describe Alice as the "Compulsive Talker" whereas John is the "Strong, Silent Type." At parties, John's happy to listen to Alice speak and she's happy to leave when he's ready to go. This difference might drive other couples batty, but for them, it works. They respect and admire each other's differences and use them to their advantage.

LESSON: If you love—or at least respect—each other's differences, you'll be a stronger couple for it.

Flexibility

You should pick a life partner the same way you'd pick a travel companion. Why? Because just like when you go on a road trip with a friend, you'll be sharing a room, most meals, and honestly most space with this person. And just as on a road trip, frustrating situations are going to come up and road blocks will slow you down, but there will also be these incredible, fun experiences. And you want to be with somebody who makes all of that—both the fun and the frustrating—*better.*

But one other way a partnership is like a road trip; your path might change. Not your destination, necessarily. You may still both want the same things. But life will throw changes at you that will force you to find a new way to get there. And inevitably, as with any adversity, you will change. You both will. And while you and your partner may not always change in the same way or at the same time, you do need to support each other. So try being flexible when differences like the following come up:

- Attitude towards work at home: one person may prefer doing work inside the house (e.g., cooking, cleaning, decorating), while the other may prefer outside work such as gardening and remodeling.
- One person may like to drive, while the other hates to drive.
- One may love to play with kids, while another may prefer to engage in adult activities.
- One partner may have a calmer temperament in dealing with difficult outsiders, while the other partner may have a shorter fuse.
- One partner may be compulsive about following their own schedule, while the other may be more flexible and accommodating.

- One partner may love being the center of attention, while the other prefers to adopt a more supportive role.

Be Dynamic

Here's a useful way to think about complementary differences. Does the way this person differs from you make situations harder for you? Or easier? If these differences don't make things easier you may want to reassess. If you're the more talkative one, then you don't need to battle for the attention of your friends when the two of you are out. If he is the more contemplative one, then he will have a solution when things go wrong. Many women envision their soul mate as someone who loves all the things they love. But the truth is, if your partner were just like you, then the two of you would have much fewer tools to use in life situations than a more dynamic couple. If you both found outsiders annoying, how would you deal with outsiders at a dinner party? The results would be kind of catastrophic. Or at the very least, there wouldn't be anyone to be friendly and to save face for the both of you. Of course, it is not always easy to know which differences will be complementary and which will simply cause tension. That depends on you and your partner and your particular differences.

Relationships Are Hard Work

Even when you find yourself in a happy, healthy relationship, that doesn't mean that everything will be "perfect."

Think of your romantic relationship the way you would think about your friendship with your best friend. Does that relationship require you put in some effort? Do you call them, make plans with them, move other things around when you know they really need your help? Do you try to hear what they have to say even when you disagree with them? All of these things require effort—which some people call work—but you know that the effort is critical to the success of your friendship. Now, what if you and that friend were always bickering, they seemed to not appreciate your efforts, and they expect you to give but they didn't see why they had to give in return? You'd probably be a little annoyed, and rightfully so. Anything that requires work should have some payoff. And to be honest, there should be a *lot* of payoff in a relationship. No matter how much work it is, the dominating feeling you have about the relationship should be *happy*. Not *okay*. And certainly not *unhappy*. But, it's important for you to realize that sometimes you have to work hard to get the happy relationship you crave. And in fact, one of the best things that you can do for your relationship is to occasionally take a step back and ask yourself a few things:

- Would I treat my best friend the way I am treating my partner?
- Am I putting too many demands or expectations on him?
- How would *you* react if your best friend were treating you the way your partner is? And, if you were unhappy with your friend's behavior, how would you address it?

By approaching your partner in this fashion, you can start to appreciate them in a different light. It'll also help you realize if you're in a relationship that's worth working for or one where it's better to cut your losses.

It's Not All Easy Street

Even the best couples can have off days. After all, you can't be completely enamoured and concerned with each other 100 percent of every day. Other parts of your life are going to interfere, upset you, excite you, and just pull you out of romance-mode. But there is nothing wrong with your partner if he is in a bad mood one day—he is only human. What matters is how he deals with his anger. Does he treat you like a confidant when he is upset, confiding in you and looking for comfort from you? Or does he take his anger out on you and make you feel like you are just an additional stress point in his life? If he does the latter, it's probably not worth it to stick around. The overall rule in any healthy relationship is to make things *easier* for your partner—and vice versa! You genuinely want to make him feel better if he is upset and you genuinely are happy for him when he's having an amazing day. So if he comes home really happy about something that happened at work, celebrate with him. If you had something you were upset about that you wanted to discuss, save it for later. Ideally, he would do the same for you.

Work as a Team When Things Get Hard

If you really don't want real life—a job, family drama, finances, mortgages, illnesses, etc.—to affect your relationship, then the two of you are best off moving to a desert island together. The reality is that a guy might be great, he might be thoughtful, he might be romantic, but what is he when something turbulent happens in your life that completely shakes your universe? And, equally important, how do you behave when life throws unexpected problems your way? If you have authentic love for your partner, you will be happy to have him there through even the most difficult situations and you'll let him know how grateful you are for his support—and he should do the same for you. In unhealthy relationships, when problems arise outside of the relationship, the couple often blames each another. This not only doesn't help solve whatever the initial problem was, but it just adds more stress. If you have a family member in the hospital, or you got fired, be warm to your partner even if it's hard and let him know you're grateful he is there. Don't become irritated at little things he does. Hopefully, when things go wrong in your life he will treat you with the same respect.

SINGLE LADIES

Whether a guy was in a fraternity in college, comes from a big family, or just loves constantly hanging out with his friends, some guys are hard to get alone! Even if he adores you, you may have a hard time weaning him off of the crew that he is always with—whether they be friends or family—so that you two can spend some alone time together and actually bond. You don't want to tell your guy that he should stop spending any time with his friends, but you should feel free to let him know that it would do your relationship some good to not have them around *all* the time. If you're starting to get serious with a guy, and even considering living with him, tell him that you wish you two had some more time together—and that all those other people who are constantly hanging out in your living room can distract the two of you from taking care of other things.

Forgiveness

Between even the most loving and honest couples, extremely hurtful things happen. Lies, affairs, even abuse. Yes, you say you would *never* stay with a man who did anything *truly* hurtful to you. But it's a whole different story when the man hurting you is the guy you thought was the love of your life. We're not going to get into when to forgive or when to walk away, but if you do make the decision to forgive, you need to stick to that. Women have a bad habit of reminding guys of everything they've done wrong—whether that be big or small. But what's the point? If you feel enough aggression towards your partner that you want to make him feel bad by constantly reminding him of his misdoings, then you should not be with him. And if you do decide to be with him, you aren't entitled to tell him off constantly. A lot of women will stay with a man who they have not forgiven, simply because they are afraid to be alone. But the healthiest thing is to make a firm decision—leave him, or be with him and forget the past. Otherwise you'll live in limbo.

Soul Mate Summary

In this chapter, you've mainly learned about compatibility, but not the chemical compatibility, which was the focus of Chapter 1. Here you dealt with the factors that create personality and emotional compatibility in couples. Here's what you should keep in mind:

The ingredients that make couples compatible include:

- Feeling comfortable and secure with one another.
- Ability to weather challenges and remain together.
- Honesty with one another.
- Kindness and caring about each other's needs.
- Enjoyment and friendship.
- Respect for each other's individuality.
- Common goals and values.
- Similar attitudes regarding family, children, and friends.
- The ability to match up on issues regarding morals, long-term goals, attitudes about family relationships, and respect for one another's intelligence.

Opposites can attract to produce complementary differences in the following areas:

- One person loves to talk; the other loves to listen.
- One partner loves housework; the other partner hates domestic activities.
- One partner enjoys activities with children; the other partner only occasionally wants to participate in these activities.

Now that you've learned how to identify a good guy and how to get him, it's time to learn how to keep him. After all, that's the ultimate goal of this book: making a quality relationship last.

CHAPTER 8

The Little Things You'll Love

Have you ever heard the phrase it's the little things that count? Well, it's true! In both life and love, the little things are what keep us smiling day in and day out. If the only good things that ever happened were grand gestures, then you would be bored most of the time and you would not recognize the small things that your partner did to show his love. Not only that, but if you are looking for a lifetime partner, you want someone who is able to enhance even the most menial moments—someone who understands your daily stresses and finds ways to make you happy in spite of them. This guy will pay attention to your life and not only try to create romantic, over-the-top moments, but will also simply try to make the difficult parts of life easier. And, if you're a single person reading this, or aren't sure you've found your Mr. Right just yet, that's okay! These things take time.

Loving You for You

A lot of times, women are impressed by the wrong things about a guy, and as a result fall for men who won't—or can't!—actually give them what they need. Meanwhile they are completely blind to the immense care and love that other men are actually showing them. You may meet a guy who fits the bill you wrote up as man of your dreams, but just remember two things: 1) Infatuation *does* fade and 2) no matter how much your friends and family compliment the handsome, well-dressed doctor boyfriend of yours, they won't be there at night in bed with the two of you. His PhD probably won't be tucked in between the sheets either.

He may be CEO of a *Fortune* 500 company, a celebrity chef, or a highly respected heart surgeon but what is he giving *you*? It doesn't matter how impressive a man is as an individual, because for the purpose of a relationship, you're not considering him merely as an individual. You're considering him as a partner, a companion, and the person who should be doing 50 percent of the work in your relationship.

The purpose of this isn't to scare you away from men. I promise. It is not to make you ultra aware of any ounce of selfishness in a man. Quite the opposite, actually. It is to make you aware of self*less*ness—of the all-important little acts of kindness—when they are right in front of you. That is, after all, the first step to a lasting and loving relationship.

SOUL MATE SCENARIOS:
Julia

Julia always veered away from what she considered a "man's man." Anyone who had a set date with the television twice a week for a football game, relentlessly turned to bathroom humor, or read car magazines —Julia immediately blocked them out and didn't give them the time of day. But one day, at a bar, she met Steve who wasn't anything that she was looking for. He was loud. He was wearing a sports jersey. She immediately decided he was a "man's man" and tried to keep their conversation short. But the wall Julia put up didn't put Steve off. He asked her questions about her career, her family, everything. And even though she was resistant to the idea of going out with him, Julia couldn't quite walk away from this guy who seemed so intent on getting to know her. So she did go on a date with him. Finally, when he had her attention (unlike at the bar when she was constantly trying to make a run for the door) Steve showed Julia more of who he was. Yes, he was a "man's man" but he was also a complete teddy bear. He had funny, unique blogs that he liked to read. He actually had studied psychology in college—a far cry from the typical sports medicine she assumed guys like Steve studied. He had no problem talking about the issues within his family, or telling her about his childhood. He even went into a topic Julia never would have pegged a "man's man" to go into—emotions. Even though Julia couldn't see Steve's capacity to have meaningful and stimulating conversations when she first met him, Steve could see that capacity in her, so he pursued her.

LESSON: Julia was lucky that Steve didn't take her initial hint at the bar and leave her alone. But not everyone will be so lucky. Not every guy will make such an effort to show who he really is to a woman who clearly isn't interested. The point is that if a man is willing to get to know you, give him a chance to show you who he is, too. Men can be more perceptive than you think. If a guy who you don't believe to be your type is pursuing you, it might be because he actually sees who you really are. If a man shows interest in you, explore that. He may have just realized that the two of you are compatible before you've come to that realization.

Telling Situations

People are multifaceted. It would be a shame to pass up on a guy who could actually make you very happy, all based on a snap judgment. It is worth your time to give him time to show you who he is. Go on a few dates in different settings. See him with his friends, in his home, with his colleagues, and—that oh so important one—with his family, or at least on the phone with his mother. You'll be surprised by the particular moments that make you realize, "Wow, I like this guy."

While it is important to remember that each man is a dynamic and unique individual, there will be times when you *should* draw on your experience with past boyfriends in order to understand someone new you are dating. Surface traits that are immediately observable like clothing, hobbies, and career shouldn't determine your judgment of a man. But there are more specific situations that can be very telling of a man's character in which it will be beneficial to compare and contrast him with past boyfriends.

THE UNIQUE TRAITS EXERCISE

Make a list of specific things past boyfriends have done that irritated you, made you angry, or made you sad. Get very specific with these situations. Example: he was rude to waitresses, he wouldn't help me make dinner, he didn't ask my friends what was happening in their lives.

_____

_____

_____

_____

_____

_____

_____

The purpose of this exercise is to recognize when a new guy does *better* in the above situations. Often, a woman will begin dating a guy who she thinks is great, but a mountain of specific things that he does will add up to an over-all feeling of dislike or disconnection. The trouble is, that feeling of dislike will often overpower the woman's ability to methodically consider where this feeling came from. All of the pain of the fighting and the disappointment will cloud her memory, and she won't sit down and think about the specific situations in which this feeling began to grow. But if you can identify the moments in which you felt disconnected from or disappointed in your ex-boyfriends, you'll be able to better recognize if you're headed down the same path with a new guy. Even if you don't think the instance in which he was rude to a waitress is the reason you two broke up, that instance in fact was significant. It was representative of a certain trait that guy had. If you look at your list, you'll probably begin to realize that each situation is representative of the same one or small group of traits. It's safe to assume that if a new guy exhibits many of the same behaviors, he has many of the same traits.

SOUL MATE SCENARIOS:
Sandy and Jeff

One evening, when attending a convention for those in the music industry, Sandy met Jeff through a mutual friend. The two got to talking and when the bar closed, Jeff mentioned that he had to excuse himself to take a business call with a client. Sandy said okay and while he was taking his call, she chatted up some of his friends who were still there.

When Jeff was done, the pair went to an after-hours spot where he told her that he definitely wanted to see her again and that there weren't very many women like her. She didn't know what he meant, but he explained that most women wouldn't have been patient enough to wait for him and chat with his friends if he had to take a business call so late at night. But, Sandy understood how their industry worked, so for her, it wasn't a big deal. And, her easygoing attitude along with some of her other traits made Jeff decide she was a keeper. Sandy did not have to pretend that she accepted Jeff's behavior. She loved it because she too had eccentric habits, and had some fear of engulfment; therefore she preferred a man like Jeff. While another woman may have felt that Jeff was neglecting her at times, Sandy welcomed the freedom the time away from Jeff afforded her. Therefore, the man who had so much difficulty finding a woman to accept his eccentricities found Sandy, who in turn, not only accepted, but appreciated his unique traits that allowed her to be herself.

LESSON: Sometimes, something that you do might seem odd to many but completely normal to those that love you. Don't tell yourself that all the good ones are taken. Someone like Jeff, who doesn't appeal to many other women, just might be that almost perfect match for you.

Women have been conditioned in so many ways to pay attention to the wrong attributes of a guy and turn a blind eye to the most important ones. Even if you have the essential ingredients, such as attraction, respect, and compatibility checked off on your relationship must-haves list—you now know him as an individual, with all of his unique traits, and he has shown that he pays attention to your unique traits, there's still a third component to consider: Biorhythms.

Biorhythms

Ready for a little more science? Research has shown that people actually have a biological rhythm. You know that friend who drives you crazy with how slowly she does everything? You could swear she applies her mascara in slow motion. It's not just that she is distracted, or obsessive-compulsive about the separation of those precious lashes, she may just be set to experience the world at a slower pace than you. All people have natural speeds: slow, medium, and fast, and just like your girlfriend's snail pace causes you to gulp down a cocktail in order to suppress your agitation, a guy can have the same effect.

Biological rhythm is not the same thing as chemistry, but it can play a large role in what you experience as chemistry. Biological rhythm makes you feel in sync with someone. Two things it has in common with chemistry: 1) you can experience it with more than one person, and 2) if it isn't there, the match probably won't last long. If you and your partner just don't live at the same speed, you'll start to feel disconnected and even agitated with one another. In the beginning, sexual attraction and the excitement of a new relationship might smooth over the tension caused by your different rhythms. For example, it may be cute that your boyfriend is ultra shy and stands quietly at your side while you are the life of the party. The saying "opposites attract" exists for a reason. But, it usually transforms into opposites creating friction, and even repelling each other.

So how can you begin to understand your own biorhythm? Start things off by taking the following quiz!

Harmony

The relationships that work out the best are usually composed of two people with similar biological rhythms. And it makes sense if you think about it. If you're the girl who stands in the middle of a party, constantly cracking jokes and keeping up witty conversation, while your guy sits in the corner nursing a beer, you just don't share experiences together. People who live at the same speed notice things on the same level, and that creates a deeper feeling of connection.

Disharmony

As we discussed in Chapter 2, sometimes you meet a man who has everything you want on paper, but for some reason the chemistry just isn't there. Sometimes this is because you two are too similar in your MHC factors, but sometimes it's also because you two have biorhythms that just don't match up. Unfortunately, these rhythms are extremely difficult—perhaps impossible —to alter, so you'd be wiser to stop trying to metaphorically force the square peg through the round hole. Try and do so and you both will only end up irritated and unhappy. The person who operates faster will become increasingly impatient while the person who is naturally slower will feel increasingly pressured until one of you snaps.

BIORHYTHM QUIZ

Answer the following questions as they best describe you.

1. You are at your best:
   a. in the morning
   b. in the afternoon or evening
   c. at night

2. You need:
   a. less than six hours of sleep
   b. less than eight hours
   c. more than eight hours

3. In your free time you prefer to:
   a. exercise
   b. do shopping or errands
   c. sit back and relax

4. Your favorite foods are:
   a. fruits and vegetables
   b. meat and starchy food
   c. foods that require time and patience to prepare

5. Your style of dress would be described as:
   a. minimal
   b. basic
   c. elaborate

6. In school you usually:
   a. sat at the front of the class, eager to speak
   b. sat in the middle
   c. sat in the back, happy to daydream

7. You often hear these words from others:
   a. slow down, please
   b. okay, let's go
   c. hurry up

8. If people complain, it's usually that you:
   a. don't smell the roses
   b. are not aware of any complaints
   c. don't get your act together

9. Your body type is:
   a. tall and thin
   b. average
   c. on the heavy side

10. I agree with which motto the most:
    a. the early bird gets the worm
    b. when in Rome, do as the Romans do
    c. I may be slow, but I am ahead of you

Scoring

Give yourself one point for every a, two points for every b, and three points for every c. Add for your total.

Interpretation

If you scored between 1 and 10, you have a fast temperament. Others may find it hard to keep up with you. If you scored between 11 and 20 your speed is average. You can be flexible and wait for the slower people or hurry for the faster people when you need to. If you scored 21 to 30, you have a slow, relaxed temperament. People like you, but sometimes get impatient with your methodical ways. If you're dating someone, you don't have to have them take the quiz, but see where you think they fall. Do the two of you match up well?

SOUL MATE SCENARIOS:
Logan

Logan and Jennifer are a classic example of opposites attracting and eventually repelling. Jennifer was extremely social, extroverted, and always the center of attention. She loved to be constantly stimulated and kept busy from the moment she woke up to the moment she went to sleep. Logan was an introvert. He liked slow mornings, sipping his coffee, and reading. He liked spending a long time wherever he went, really taking in the experience. Logan was drawn to Jennifer's vivacity. She brought excitement into his quiet life. Jennifer was drawn to Logan's peaceful temperament. He brought serenity to her busy life. At dinner parties Jennifer did most of the talking, constantly making people laugh, while Logan sat quietly at her side holding her hand. Logan liked that Jennifer embodied traits that he did not have, and vice versa. But, there were only so many mornings Jennifer was content curled up on the couch while Logan read. She grew anxious. She'd constantly look over his shoulder, asking when they could leave and start the day. Logan grew tired of going to parties with Jennifer. He became irritated and even cold towards other guests at the party, resenting Jennifer for putting him in situations where he had to be social when he just didn't feel like it. In the end, even though they both wished they were a little bit more like one another, they simply were not and could not be because one's biological rhythm is almost impossible to change.

LESSON: Before taking your vows make sure you and your partner have the same or similar biorhythms. It'll save you heartache down the line.

Can you see how important these compatibility factors are to maintaining a relationship, as opposed to the soul mate myth? There is nothing that makes two people feel more connected than feeling that they experience things the same way, make the same observations, and even feel the same level of satisfaction after an experience. You both might notice that one of your friends was distracted during dinner one night or that two of your friends were hitting it off. Again, these are random and specific situations, but these are the things that create a feeling of connection. If his response to most of your observations is, "Huh, I didn't notice that," then you probably don't have similar biological rhythms.

Soul Mate Summary

You love your partner, but sometimes you may forget to appreciate him and make him feel as though he's number one in your life (after you, of course!) Throughout this chapter, you should have learned some ways to go the extra mile for the one you care so much about. Here's a little recap of what you should take away:

- The important and small things such as compatible eccentricities can turn a seemingly undesirable man into one you find to be quite loveable.

- Biorhythms are genetically determined relationships to time and space, which cause a person to be comfortable with either a slow-paced, medium, or fast-paced activity level. This elusive factor can be a deal-breaker or a deal-maker in a long-term relationship.

- You need to give a person time to display all his personal qualities. As you get to know one another, you can appreciate qualities in your partner, and vice versa, that are unique to the two of you.

There are many little things that you can do to show your partner how much you appreciate him in his uniqueness. We've explored some of the small ways that you can demonstrate your love for one another. Now you're on your way to a relationship that is grounded in reality rather than fantasy—and that's a great thing!

Love a Man, Not a Myth

Congratulations! You've come a long way. When you began reading this book, you believed that there was an ideal man known as your soul mate out there waiting for you. You were frustrated because you had not yet met this mythical creature. But you've learned a lot while you've been reading, including:

- The factors that science has proven account for attraction and maintenance of a love relationship. Chemistry and biology has been proven to play a larger part in your choice of mate than the soul mate myth.
- Which expectations are reasonable for a long-term partner, and which of your old expectations are unrealistic.
- How to become open and flexible to different men.
- There is no such thing as an ideal partner; and you do not need to be stuck dating only "your type."
- What you really need from a man, and what it takes to have your needs met.

So whether you have had difficulty getting a date, have been frustrated with the men you were dating, or are in a relationship but don't know if they guy you're with is the right guy for you, you now have a toolkit that will help you work out these issues. You are now ready to hit the road and you are well prepared for the journey.

Some of the lessons that you've learned throughout *The Soul Mate Myth* have likely sent you into a little bit of a tailspin. And whether your guy knows it or not, you've put him through a lot of "tests" to figure out if the two of you are compatible. But even if your guy got a check mark on *every* trait we've discussed, if you don't *feel* totally crazy about him, then what does it matter? If you are presently involved with a man, and you want to measure the intensity of your feelings for him, take the following quiz.

IS IT TRUE LOVE? QUIZ

Answer the following questions true or false as they apply to your relationship with your partner.

1. If he is gone for even a few days, I miss him very much.   True   False

2. I sometimes feel a rush to my head when I think of seeing him.
   True   False

3. I find that when he's in distress, I worry about him.   True   False

4. I know that when I have a terrible problem he's the person that I go to before anyone else.   True   False

5. I would have no problem making a commitment to my partner.
   True   False

6. He enhances my life in many ways.   True   False

7. I feel happy and think of him whenever I see a romantic scene.
   True   False

8. I talk about him very often to my family and friends.   True   False

9. I often buy little gifts for him just because it's what I want to do.
   True   False

10. I often feel the need to call or check in with him.   True   False

11. I trust that he is not cheating on me because we have such a wonderful relationship.   True   False

Scoring
Give your self one point for each true and zero points for each false.

Interpretation
If you scored 9 to 11, congratulations, it looks like this has all the elements of a good relationship. Trust, warmth, love, commitment, and concern for the well-being for the other person. If you scored 6 to 8, you have most of the elements of a good long-term relationship. He still has the potential to develop into being the one Mr. Right. If you scored 0 to 5, it appears that this relationship is more on a casual level as far as you are concerned. You enjoy being together but you do not feel a sense of long-term commitment.

Honestly though, in the long run, the score you—or your guy—received on this last quiz doesn't really matter. You're don't have to be stuck with someone that you don't feel passionately about. Now that you've said goodbye to the idea of the soul mate, the possibilities of finding a great guy are endless. Even if you're having trouble finding someone or are in a relationship that you've realized won't last, you've learned how to broaden your horizons. And who knows, the right guy for you might be right over the next hill. Have fun and good luck!

The Single Girl's Dating Guide

Whether you're new to the dating scene or just haven't had much luck for a while, you're probably wondering just how you meet great guys . . . because even though you have realistic expectations, you have yet to come across one of these great guys we've been talking about.

Where Are the Men?

Though it may not seem like it sometimes, men *are* everywhere. But that doesn't mean you should necessarily be looking *everywhere*. Remember how you can't just wait for the perfect man to waltz into your life? That you have to make your life what you want it to be by doing everything that makes you happy. The guy who is attracted to you while you're happy is the one you want to be with. Start looking at the activities you personally enjoy as places to also meet someone. You may have thought before that the daytime was for doing things you love with your girlfriends and the night time was for looking for guys at bars. Combine those two worlds. If you love hiking, taking cocktail-making classes, salsa dancing—whatever it may be—do that and do it a lot! If you don't meet a guy there who is interested in the same things you are, you will at least make friends through whom you have a better chance of meeting a good guy. Do the things that make you happy. There is nothing more attractive to a guy than a girl who takes control of her life and does the things she loves. But the work doesn't *completely* stop with having fun and waiting to attract someone. When he does approach, you need to flirt.

Flirting Basics

You might be thinking "but I'm *not* a flirt!" First off, stop thinking that flirting is so taboo. Second, there are a million ways to flirt. You don't have to be just like that one friend of yours who is always uncomfortably aggressive towards guys just because you want to flirt. You can set your own flirting style. But you do need to let a guy know you're interested. This isn't a job interview. This person wants to know if you are someone he can *enjoy* his time with. Look at flirting this way—you want to make the interaction fun for you. That means making jokes that make *you* laugh. Talking about things that make *you* happy. And, of course, throwing a little compliment in there doesn't hurt.

Here is the great thing about guys—they don't reject a woman's advances nearly as much as women reject men's. Be honest, when a guy first approaches you, he usually has to work his way up to even having your attention. When a woman approaches a man, she usually has his attention from the get-go. If the guy you've approached has a girlfriend or just isn't interested, he just won't ask for your number. That's about the worst that could happen.

Here are a few things you can do to show a guy you're interested:

- Look him directly in the eye and then coyly glance away or saunter by him.
- Laugh naturally at his jokes (men who are interested want to impress you, and one of the main ways they try to do this is through humor. This also shows you have a sense of humor, which is really important because sometimes women can seem a little too serious).
- Compliment him on his clothing, his hair, his knowledge of something or another, etc. Do this subtly though and get him to allow you to compliment him. For example, if he says he loves a certain actor's style, say "I picked up on that."
- Ask him to help you do something (such as reach that thing on the top shelf in the supermarket). It sounds cliché, but guys love to be thought of as the capable man you can turn to. It boosts their ego. The moment you ask a guy for help, he can't help but view himself as your protector for at least a brief moment.
- Touch him lightly on the arm or the shoulder when you're talking to him.
- Gently tease him; it shows you have a good sense of humor.

If you follow this advice, the guy you're flirting with will probably take the hint and ask you out. But what should you do when that happens?

The First Date

So, a guy you like finally asked you out. Now, where to go? What to do? Most likely, he'll take charge of this, but just in case he doesn't here are a few ideas:

- **Meet for Lunch or Coffee:** If you're not sure you're going to definitely like the guy (let's say it's a blind date or a guy you met online), meeting for lunch or coffee means that you'll have a shorter date than if you met for dinner. Also, even with your best intentions, it's too easy to have one too many drinks on a dinner or drinks date, and this could greatly alter the way you perceive the guy. You might think you *really* like him because you're, well, *really* tipsy. Start with a casual daytime date. If things go well, you can always stay longer, and if things don't, you can use the excuse that you need to meet a friend or get back to work.
- **Do Something:** While going to a film on a first date may not be a great idea because you can't talk to each other, going on a hike or to the zoo or a museum or somewhere where you can both be actively or intellectually engaged can be a lot of fun. You'll get to see what he's like "in the wild" so to speak and participating in an activity gives you more to talk about than the usual, "So where are you from?" stuff.

These activities are good ones for beginning a relationship when you are uncertain about pursuing it further. They are non-threatening, comfortable activities, to give both of you a chance to warm up to one another.

What to Wear

You might be surprised to hear this, but men don't really care what women wear on a first date. Now, they're not blind and they will notice if you're particularly fashion forward, sexy, sporty, whatever. They'll *notice* it, but it won't be what *attracts* them to you. The only thing that matters about your outfit is that you are comfortable in it. If you feel confident in what you're wearing, whether it's a cute shirt, jeans, and heels or a dress or anything in between, the guy you're going out with will notice.

And, as far as makeup is concerned, don't go overboard with that either. According to a study on *OkCupid.com*, 75 percent of men who responded said they'd prefer to go on a date with a woman who wears minimal, natural looking makeup (if any). So, leave the airbrushing and the glamour shots to the magazines. Besides, if things progress and you eventually wake up with him, he'll find out what you really look like.

One more thing: don't show too much skin. Guys like a little mystery, so pick one aspect of your body to highlight. That means wear a sexy skirt or a low-cut top if you so desire, but not both. Remember, the key is to be comfortable, laid-back, and fun.

Dating Etiquette

Etiquette is one of the most important factors in creating a good impression. This is what you are aiming to do on a first date. If you are someone who loves to drink yard-long cocktails and ride the mechanical bull, terrific, but the first date isn't necessarily the best time to show him that side of you. No matter how wild a person you are, being polite fits into every personality type. So say thank you when he opens the door, pays for the meal, or puts your jacket on for you. Let him know who you are, but don't display it all at once. And, as stated before, take it easy on the alcohol on a first date. More than two drinks and you just won't be your best, sharp, witty self.

Don't Be Late

It's a very important date, right? Then show the guy you're meeting that you're excited to see him and that you respect him and show up on time. Leave yourself extra time to get there so that you don't show up stressed when you inevitably run into traffic or spend ten extra minutes trying to find your car keys. Also, since a lot of women have trouble with punctuality, this gives you an advantage.

Pay Your Way

Even though it's customary for a man to pay for the first date, it is still polite of you to offer. He'll probably turn you down, but he'll definitely appreciate the gesture. On the second date you can follow the lead that he established previously. You don't need to offer to pay if he paid for the first date. Then, if you really like him, pay for at least part of the third date. At the very least, he'll realize that you aren't trying to take advantage of his generosity.

DID YOU KNOW?

Despite women's strength in the workforce, 42 percent of women still think men should always pay for the date.

Smile

It may not seem like brain surgery, but you definitely don't want to come across as super serious on a date. This isn't a job interview, so have fun! Flirt, smile, and show that you're a pleasure to be around. Also, indicate that you are enjoying the date. He is probably as nervous as you are about making a good impression. He wants to know that you are having a good time, especially if he is the one who chose the activity. If you smile, he's likely to smile back at you too; and if he's having fun, your chances of a second date or a long-term relationship increase.

Know When to Say Goodnight

If you want to keep a guy coming back, it's important to realize when the date is over and not prolong a date past it's natural end. This definitely means not going home with him on the first date. Also, unless you are just *so* incredibly deep in conversation that you can't possibly stop talking now, don't suggest you go do something else immediately after, like go to a bar next to the restaurant to keep things going. Save that for next time. This keeps him feeling like he's pursuing you and not the other way around.

Also, don't call or text him right away. Instead, wait for him to reach out. Remember the above suggestion so that you don't appear desperate. However, do not be so "hard to get" that you appear disinterested. Take it one step at a time, depending upon his reaction. A confident man may enjoy chasing you a bit, while a shy guy may be put off by any sign of rejection. Feel it out based on the particular guy.

Watch His Body Language

If you can "read" your date by observing his body language, you have a distinct advantage. You can adjust your behavior according to the nonverbal feedback that his body language provides you. Is he interested? Is he looking you in the eyes while you speak or eyeing the menu, or his phone, or another girl? Is he leaned intently towards you or is he more nonchalant, leaned back, and just waiting until he can end the date and go do something else? These signs will give you a clue to which way he's leaning about you:

- He's been genuinely smiling throughout the date and laughing at your jokes or gently teasing you. That means his smile doesn't look forced, his eyes are crinkling, and both sides look about the same.
- His feet are pointed towards you. Without thinking about it, we tend to turn our feet towards the direction we want to go. That means if his are facing the door instead of you, things aren't going so well.
- He touches you. This one should be pretty obvious, but if he's touching you, he's interested. If he pushes your hair back, that means he's feeling protective of you, which is a great sign he's interested in more than just sex.
- He plays with his belt or belt loops. This usually indicates he's thinking about sex, so it definitely means he's attracted. But if he crosses his legs or tries to hide his genitals in one way or another, that may mean the opposite.

Work Your Body Language

Since you want to be sure that you are giving your date the right signals, here are some pointers regarding your own body language.

- Smile with your eyes as well as your mouth. Keep your facial expression relaxed and happy.
- Maintain eye contact to show interest in his conversation.
- Keep hand gestures light and appropriate. Remember, you do not want to appear loud and excessive.
- Keep your voice level within the moderate range.
- Laughter is great because it shows that you are enjoying the date, but don't be excessively giggly or loud.
- Display energy and vitality. Do not appear tired, bored, or overly agitated.

If you follow the above pointers, you will be the most helpful to yourself in making a good impression. This will increase the probability that he will feel comfortable and wish to pursue the relationship further.

Online Dating

Okay, so now you know it's better not to focus too much on superficial desires and give the men you meet the benefit of the doubt and not be fooled by first impressions. But, what do you do when it comes to online dating? After all, 40 million Americans are doing it, so why shouldn't you?

With the exception of a few sites that require you to take a test and then match you up on what they think are the key factors that would make you two compatible in real life, most let you choose which characteristics you'd like to see in your "perfect guy." There are at least two major problems with this. The first is that you're likely to end up basing your choices almost entirely on looks alone. And, with all of the guys on the site to pick from, why not choose the handsomest? Well, there's a chance that these guys aren't always going to be the best match for you. It's not that you won't end up with a guy who could be a male model, but just take a look at all of your past boyfriends. Were all of them model material? Probably not. Did you find them attractive? Probably. You shouldn't go out with a guy who you find unattractive, but don't turn someone down because they're not a perfect ten either.

The second issue is that, in this modern-day world where almost everyone engages in e-mail, texting, and social networking, who we are online isn't always who we are in person. Forget the extreme cases of fifty-something-year-old guys pretending to be successful twenty-seven-year-old stockbrokers because, in those cases, you should trust the old adage that if it seems too good to be true it probably is. But while you and a guy might have a good rapport online, you can't see his body language, you don't know how long it took him to write that e-mail that caught your eye (was it his first draft or did he spend a half hour working on it until it read perfectly?), etc. It's been said that 7 percent of our communication is verbal and *93 percent* is nonverbal. So, really, online you're only getting to see 7 percent of what this guy is like. No wonder you don't know if you have chemistry! Not to mention you don't know how your MHC factors and pheromones line up. So, pick a site or two to host your profile on and send a few e-mails back and forth with the guys you're interested in. But, don't wait long until you see if there's real chemistry in person.

Post an Interesting Photo

Men are visual creatures, so a captivating photo is the best way to attract them. Make sure you have a least one photo where you're looking directly at the camera—or even your camera phone. Just keep in mind that the key is to look laid-back, flirtatious, and fun. You've heard this before, but if you seem like a fun, laid-back woman you'll be that much more successful in the dating game.

Write a Captivating Profile

While it's true that men choose women mostly based on their photos, if you have a great photo but a bad profile, you probably won't get very many dates. Try your best to capture your unique personality in your profile. Talk about your interests, your passions, trips you've enjoyed, etc. The most important thing you can do is be honest but also come across as a fun person to be around.

Writing That Introductory E-mail

Keep it short and sweet. Flirt! Don't make a list of all the things you like about him, but pick one aspect and ask about that, or just tease him in a cute way. Basically, you just want to let him know you're interested but encourage him to make the first real move. It's the equivalent of catching his eye at a party and then looking away. In the end, it is up to you to attract and maintain good relationships.

So congratulations! You have learned much about the science and art of attraction, romance, and long-term love. Practice and apply what you have learned. You can refer back to suggestions, tests, and exercises in the previous chapters as needed. Great relationships are in your future.

Resource List

While I'd love for this book to be *the* be-all, end-all guide to finding Mr. Right, there are other sources out there that may be of use to you in your quest.

Websites

www.prepare-enrich.com – This program helps premarital couples prepare for marriage and helps married couples enrich their relationship.

www.gottman.com – The Gottman Institute applies the latest research on marriage to cognitive behavioral therapy and is based upon research on why many marriages succeed or fail.

www.APA.org/relationships – The American Psychological Association help site provides many resources in terms of links, books, research papers, and referral to treatment centers.

www.aamft.org – The American Association for Marriage and Family Therapy helps you find a marriage or family therapist in your area.

www.parentswithoutpartners.org – Parents Without Partners provides single parents with opportunities for support, friendship, and activities with other single parents.

www.helpguide.org/mental/improve – This is a great tool to help you learn how to build relationships deep in emotional intelligence.

Where to Go for Help If You're in an Abusive Relationship

www.domesticviolence.org – This site provides information about many local resources.

www.ovc.gov – This site provides links to many resources that can be helpful in fighting domestic violence.

www.feminist.org/911/crisis.html – This site provides details of organizations offering help to victims in the United States.

www.silcom.com – A domestic violence website that provides access to hotlines and services throughout the United States.

Books and Publications

Fisher, Helen (2009). *Why Him? Why Her?: Finding Real Love by Understanding Your Personality Type.* New York: Henry Holt and Company.

Fisher, Helen (2004). *Why We Love: The Nature and Chemistry of Romantic Love.* New York: Henry Holt and Company.

Fisher, Helen (1992). *Anatomy of Love: A Natural History of Mating, Marriage and Why We Stray.* London: Quill.

Gottman, John (2009). *Why Marriages Succeed or Fail—And How You Can Make Yours Last.* New York: Sterling.

Kasl, Charlotte (2005). *Women, Sex, and Addiction: A Search for Love and Power.* New York: Hyperion.

Naumann, Earl (2001). *Love at First Sight: The Stories and Science Behind Instant Attraction.* Chicago: Sourcebooks Casablanca.

Norwood, Robin (1985). *Women Who Love Too Much*. New York: Penguin Publishing.

Pincott, Jena (2008). *Do Gentlemen Really Prefer Blondes?* New York: Random House.

Pines, A.M (1999). *Falling in Love: Why We Choose the Lovers We Choose*. London: Routledge.

Schaeffer, Brenda (2008). *Is It Love or Is It Addiction?* New York: Random House.

Index

Commitment fears quiz, 88

Communication quiz, 169–71

Communication skills, 28–29, 167–74

Compatibility
affection, 21–23
companionship, 21
conflicts, 23–25
emotional compatibility, 17–25, 186–90, 202
fidelity, 18
respect, 17–18
sexual compatibility, 18–20
trust, 18
values, 23–24

Complementary differences, 194, 202

Compromise, 26–29, 83, 174, 185–86

Conclusions, jumping to, 73

Conflict resolution, 23–25, 172–75

Conflict resolution quiz, 175

Cultural barriers, 124–25

D

Dating
attire for, 225
etiquette for, 225–27
first dates, 8, 224–25
guide for, 221–31
online dating, 229–31
saying goodnight, 227

studies on, 16

Dating guide, 221–31

Dehydroepiandrosterone (DHEA), 40–41

Depression, 147–50

"Desire neurotransmitter," 44

Differences, accepting, 26

Differences, complementary, 194, 202

Discussions, 28–29. *See also* Communication skills

Disharmony, 210

Do Gentlemen Really Prefer Blondes?, 52

Dopamine, 42, 44, 57, 59

Drama, 160

Dynamics, 197

E

Eccentricities, 208, 215

Ellis, Havelock, 34

Emotional compatibility, 17–25, 186–90, 202. *See also* Compatibility

Endorphins, 43

Engulfment fears, 79–85. *See also* Fears

Engulfment fears quiz, 82

Estrogen, 37–39, 47

Estrogen quiz, 38–39

Etiquette, 225–29. *See also* Dating

Expectations

P

"Passion chemical," 44
"Perfect man"
  constructing, 116–17
  grieving for, 137–53
  type of, 117–18
"Perfect relationship," 5, 8–9,
  157. *See also* Relationships
Personalization, 70–71
Phenylethylamine (PEA),
  43–44, 57, 59
Pheromones, 40, 62
Physical characteristic barrier,
  122–23
Pincott, Jena, 52
Plato, 14
Positives, discounting, 72–73
Prescription enhancements,
  47. *See also* Love
  enhancements
Pressure, 161–64
Pride and Prejudice, 4
Professional help, 149
Progesterone, 40

Q

Quizzes
  abandonment fears quiz, 99
  biorhythm quiz, 211–12
  commitment fears quiz, 88
  communication quiz,
    169–71
  conflict resolution quiz, 175

engulfment fears quiz, 82
estrogen quiz, 38–39
good-match quiz, 189
novelty fears quiz, 108
rational thinking quiz,
  74–77
rejection fears quiz, 104
true love quiz, 219
vulnerability quiz, 94

R

Rational thinking, 74–77
Reality check, 1
Reasonable expectations,
  15–16
Reasonable needs, 119–22
Rejection fears, 101–6
Rejection fears quiz, 104
Relationships. *See also* Life
  partner
  abusive relationships, 161–
    63, 200–201, 234
  authentic relationships,
    157–84
  expectations of, 1, 3–32
  fears of, 78–85
  long-term relationships, 26,
    31, 45–46, 133–37, 157
  main ingredients of,
    185–202
  "perfect relationship," 5,
    8–9, 157
  working at, 197–200

About the Author

Jean Cirillo, PhD, obtained her BA in psychology from New York University. She then received two master's degrees from Columbia University in psychology and counseling. She later obtained her doctoral degree in clinical and school psychology from Hofstra University. She has more than twenty-five years of experience as a counselor and staff psychologist. With a strong background in family and marital counseling, she has treated patients individually; served as an expert consultant to schools, news programs, talk shows, and documentaries; and overseen treatment teams in a hospital setting. She has served on the executive boards in both the Nassau County and the New York State Psychological Association, and served one term as president of the New York State Psychological Association's Division of Women's Issues. As *The Jenny Jones Show*'s staff psychologist, she gave advice, follow-up counseling, and aftercare referrals for guests of the program. She lives in Huntington, NY. Check her out at *www.drjeantv.net*.